Capital Markets and Securities Laws

Capital Markets and Securities Laws

E.T. Lokganathan

Associate Professor,
Department of Corporate Secretaryship and
Professional Accounting,
Kongu Arts and Science College, Erode, Tamil Nadu

New Century Publications
New Delhi, India

NEW CENTURY PUBLICATIONS
4800 / 24, Bharat Ram Road,
Ansari Road, Daryaganj,
New Delhi - 110 002 (India)

Tel.: 011-2324 7798, 4358 7398, 4101 7798

E-mail: info@newcenturypublications.com

www.newcenturypublications.com

Editorial office:
LG – 7, Aakarshan Bhawan,
4754-57/23, Ansari Road, Daryaganj,
New Delhi – 110 002

Tel.: 011-4356 0919

First Published: **2019**

ISBN: **978-81-7708-493-1**

Published by New Century Publications and printed at Milan Enterprises, New Delhi.

Designs: Patch Creative Unit, New Delhi.

PRINTED IN INDIA

About the Book

Prior to the initiation of financial reforms in the early 1990s, capital market structure in India was subject to several controls and opaque procedures. The trading and settlement system was outdated and not in tune with international practices. Raising of capital from the market was regulated by the Capital Issues (Control) Act, 1947 which was administered by the Controller of Capital Issues (CCIs) in the Ministry of Finance, Government of India. The scheme of controls under the Act required all the companies to obtain prior consent for issue of capital to the public. Pricing as well as the features of the capital structure (such as debt-equity ratios), were controlled by the Government.

The Securities Contracts (Regulation) Act, 1956 was administered by the Directorate of Stock Exchanges, also in the Ministry of Finance. It empowered the Government to recognise/derecognise stock exchanges, stipulate rules and by-laws for their functioning, compel listing of securities by public companies etc. Such a system of regulation and control was fragmented and inadequate in the context of liberalisation wave sweeping across the world. Urgent measures were needed to relax controls and modernise the functioning of capital market.

It was in this backdrop, that wide-ranging financial sector reforms in India were introduced as an integral part of the economic reforms process started in the early 1990s. Reforms in respect of capital markets have focused on creating a deregulated environment and enabling free play of market forces while at the same time strengthening the prudential norms and the supervisory system.

Part I of this book, containing 10 chapters, explains and examines at length the structure of capital markets in India. Part II of the book, comprising 9 chapters, provides basic knowledge about securities laws and related matters.

About the Author

Dr. E.T. Lokganathan is Associate Professor, Department of Corporate Secretaryship and Professional Accounting, Kongu Arts and Science College, Erode, Tamil Nadu. He did his M.Phil. and Ph.D. from Alagappa University, Tamil Nadu. He is also an MBA and PGDCA from the same university.

With 19 years of teaching and research experience, he has published a good number of papers in peer reviewed journals. He was awarded the Certificate of Excellence in Education by the Rotary Club of Erode.

Dr. Lokganathan has presented 25 papers at national level and 8 papers at international level seminars and conferences. He is a member of Board of Studies in Corporate Secretaryship, Bharathiar University, Coimbatore. He has also authored a book titled *Intellectual Property Rights (IPRs): TRIPS Agreement and Indian Laws*. His area of specialization is corporate laws.

Contents

Part II: Securities Laws

Preface

Till the initiation of economic reforms in early 1990s, financial markets in India were characterised by control over pricing of financial assets, barriers to entry, high transaction costs and restrictions in movement of funds between the market segments. This, apart from inhibiting the development of the markets, also affected their efficiency.

Capital market structure was subject to several controls and opaque procedures. The trading and settlement system was outdated and not in tune with international practices. Raising of capital from the market was regulated by the Capital Issues (Control) Act, 1947 which was administered by the Controller of Capital Issues (CCIs) in the Ministry of Finance, Government of India. The scheme of controls under the Act required all the companies to obtain prior consent for issues of capital to the public. Pricing as well as the features of the capital structure (such as debt-equity ratios), were controlled by the Government.

The Securities Contracts (Regulation) Act, 1956 was administered by the Directorate of Stock Exchanges, also in the Ministry of Finance. It empowered the Government to recognise/derecognise stock exchanges, stipulate rules and by-laws for their functioning, compel listing of securities by public companies etc. Such a system of regulation and control was fragmented and inadequate in the context of liberalisation wave sweeping across the world. Urgent measures were needed to relax controls and modernise the functioning of capital market.

It was in this backdrop, that wide-ranging financial sector reforms in India were introduced as an integral part of the economic reforms process initiated in the early 1990s. Reforms in respect of financial intermediaries and financial markets have focused on creating a deregulated environment and enabling free play of market forces while at the same time strengthening the prudential norms and the supervisory system.

Financial sector reforms since the early 1990s have focused on the following objectives: (a) elimination of segmentation across various markets in order to facilitate transmission of impulses across markets, (b) easing the liquidity management process, and (c) making resource allocation more efficient across the economy.

Further, reforms in the financial markets have been undertaken within the overall monetary policy framework and in co-ordination with reforms in the money and foreign exchange markets. Many of the major reforms have been implemented in phases, allowing for transition so as not to destabilise market conditions or any group of participants or the financial system in general.

Financial sector reforms have paved the way for integration among various segments of the financial system. It is widely accepted that reduction/removal of financial repression has enhanced the efficiency and potential growth of the Indian economy.

Erode **E.T. Lokganathan**

Part I

Capital Markets

1

Indian Capital Market: An Introduction

1.1 Meaning and Importance of Capital Market

Capital market is a market for long-term funds. The distinction between capital market and money market is not watertight. Broadly speaking, capital market focuses on financing of fixed investment (machinery and equipment) while money market provides working capital finance (raw material etc.).

Capital market channelises household savings to the corporate sector and allocates funds to firms. In this process, it allows both firms and households to share risks associated with business. Moreover, capital market enables the valuation of firms on an almost continuous basis and plays an important role in the governance of the corporate sector.

An efficient capital market is an important constituent of a sound financial system. In India, efforts have been made in recent years to set up an effective regulatory framework covering major participants in the capital market. Similarly, the technology of trading and settlements in the stock exchanges has been upgraded. Internet-based trading in securities has been permitted. Foreign institutional investors (FIIs) and pension funds were allowed to enter the Indian stock market from 1993 onwards. The market has undergone a major transformation in terms of its structure, products, practices, spread, institutional framework and other important aspects like transparency, integrity and efficiency since then. The size of the market has also grown manifold.

Capital market fosters economic growth in following ways:

1. It augments the quantum of savings and capital formation in the economy.
2. It allocates capital efficiently thereby raising the

productivity of investment.

3. It enhances the efficiency of a financial system as diverse competitors vie with each other for financial resources.
4. It adds to the financial deepening of the economy by enlarging the financial sector and promoting the use of innovative, sophisticated and cost-effective financial instruments, which ultimately reduce the cost of capital.
5. Well-functioning capital markets also impose discipline on firms to perform.
6. Equity and debt markets stress on the banking sector by diversifying credit risk across the economy.

1.2 Evolution of Capital Market in India

Capital market structure has evolved over time with the market practices and conditions generally reflecting the policies put in place. Till the onset of reforms in the early 1990s, raising of resources in the primary segment of the market was subject to several controls, disallowing pricing to be determined by market conditions. Trading in the secondary market was subject to opaque practices. The trading and settlement system was outdated and out of tune with internationally followed practices. The volumes, however, increased and securities continued to exist in physical form. Physical securities also created uncertainties for investors and increased the transaction costs. Besides, long and uncertain settlement cycles created serious problems for clearing houses. Informational flows to the market participants were also deficient. It was considered necessary to orient the SEBI to undertake the tasks of regulation and supervision. The SEBI was, for this purpose, given statutory powers through a separate legislation in 1992.

Although the capital market in India has a long history, during the most part, it remained on the periphery of the financial system. Various reforms undertaken since the early 1990s by the Securities and Exchange Board of India (SEBI) and the Government have brought about a significant structural transformation in the Indian capital market. As a result, the

Indian equity market has become modern and transparent.

The improvement in clearing and settlement system has brought a substantial reduction in transaction costs. Several measures were also undertaken to enhance the safety and integrity of the market. These include capital requirements, trading and exposure limits, daily margins comprising mark-to-market margins and VaR based margins. Trade/settlement guarantee fund has also been set up to ensure smooth settlement of transactions in case of default by any member. Another important development of the reform process was the opening up of mutual funds industry to the private sector in 1992, which earlier was the monopoly of the Unit Trust of India (UTI) and mutual funds set up by public sector financial institutions.

Since 1992, foreign institutional investors (FIIs) are permitted to invest in all types of securities, including corporate debt and government securities in stages and subject to limits. Further, the Indian corporate sector was allowed to access international capital markets through American depository receipts (ADRs), global depository receipts (GDRs), foreign currency convertible bonds (FCCBs) and external commercial borrowings (ECBs). Eligible foreign companies have been permitted to raise money from domestic capital markets through issue of Indian depository receipts (IDRs).

Regulations governing substantial acquisition of shares and takeovers of companies have also been put in place. These are aimed at making the takeover process more transparent and to protect the interests of minority shareholders.

To sustain confidence in clearing and settlement of securities, NSE set up the National Securities Clearing Corporation Ltd. (NSCCL) in August 1995 which carries out the clearing and settlement of the trades executed in the equities and derivatives segments and operates the subsidiary general ledger (SGL) for settlement of trades in government securities. Similarly, the BSE has its own clearing house.

The equity market has witnessed widespread development in

infrastructure and its functioning is comparable to international standards. It has seen significant increase in growth and diversity in composition since early 1990s.

Trading infrastructure in the stock exchanges has been modernised by replacing the open outcry system with online screen-based electronic trading. This has improved the liquidity in the Indian capital market and led to better price discovery. The trading and settlement cycles were initially shortened from 14 days to 7 days. Subsequently, to enhance the efficiency of the secondary market, rolling settlement was introduced on a T+5 basis. With effect from April 1, 2002, the settlement cycle for all listed securities was shortened to T+3 and further to T+2 from April 1, 2003. Shortening of settlement cycles helped in reducing risks associated with unsettled trades due to market fluctuations.

As a result of these initiatives, there has been a significant rise in the volume of transactions and the emergence of new and innovative instruments. In addition to the three permanent stock exchanges, viz., the NSE, BSE, and the Calcutta Stock Exchange Ltd., the 3 other prominent ones include India International Exchange (India INX), Metropolitan Stock Exchange of India Ltd. and NSE IFSC Ltd. Small regional stock exchanges have been granted exit by SEBI vide different orders.

1.3 Issues and Concerns

The role of equity market in capital formation continues to be limited. The private corporate debt market is active mainly in the form of private placements, while the public issue market for corporate debt is yet to pick up. It is the primary equity and debt markets that link the issuers of securities and investors and provide resources for capital formation. A growing economy requires risk capital and long-term resources in the form of debt for enabling the corporates to choose an appropriate mix of debt and equity. Long-term resources are also important for financing infrastructure projects. Therefore, in order to sustain India's high growth path, the capital market needs to play a major role. The significance of a well-functioning domestic capital market has also increased as banks need to raise necessary capital from the market to sustain their growing operations.

A major issue which will influence India's securities markets in the future is the challenge of globalisation. RBI has increasingly moved in the direction of giving access to international diversification to institutional investors and individual investors in India. Financial intermediaries and exchanges in India will also experience global competition. There is a need for fully integrating a global perspective into the plans of firms, exchanges, regulators and policy makers.

The Indian capital market has become modern in terms of market infrastructure and trading and settlement practices. The capital market has also become a much safer place than it was before the reform process began. The secondary capital market in India has also become deep and liquid. There has also been a reduction in transaction costs and significant improvement in efficiency and transparency. However, the role of the domestic capital market in capital formation in the country, both directly and indirectly through mutual funds, continues to be less significant.

Post-liberalization, the Indian stock market witnessed a number of scams due to which small investors are reluctant to enter the market. History has witnessed how regulators remained mute spectators, allowing brokers to trap investors. If the government wants investors back in the capital market, it needs to strengthen the regulators, make them efficient, accountable and investor-friendly. In the current scenario of volatile stock market, which is now a fact of life in the globalised economy, investors have to be on their toes and take proactive decisions. They cannot be docile investors, either be active or be out of business. They should not take the market as a place for speculators and punters. In civilized societies, the law and legal system are supposed to protect the interests of those who lend and not those who fail to repay.

To sum up, the capital market has been an important source

of funding for larger companies and the opening of the economy to portfolio flows from foreign institutional investors (FIIs). In recent years, it has produced a buoyant capital market where companies have raised significant funds through new issues. However, this mechanism has been used mainly by the larger companies to raise funds. There are no effective institutions that can channel equity funding to smaller companies and start-ups. In a knowledge economy, there is need to encourage the growth of venture capital funds and angel investors.

2

Capital Market Reforms in India

Historically, different kinds of financial intermediaries have existed in the Indian financial system. At the time of Independence in 1947, working capital requirements of corporates were financed mainly by commercial banks. As the capital market was underdeveloped, a number of development finance institutions (DFIs) were set up at the all-India and the State levels to meet the long-term fund requirements of companies.

2.1 Capital Market in the Pre-reforms (i.e. Pre-1991) Period

Prior to the onset of financial sector reforms in 1991, the capital market structure in India was subject to several controls and opaque procedures. The objective of control over capital issues was to channel the limited capital resources available for investment in the country into desired areas. Apart from this main objective, capital issues control was put to several other uses, these being the following:

1. Regulation of bonus issues.
2. Regulation of terms and conditions of foreign capital participation in Indian companies and the regulation of the terms and conditions of dilution or repatriation of foreign equity.
3. Regulation of capital re-organisation plans of companies, including mergers and amalgamations.
4. Regulation of the capital structure of companies, as well as the terms and conditions of additional issues.
5. Regulation of the volume and timing of the private issue of capital.

Moreover, the trading and settlement system was outdated and not in tune with international practices. Raising of capital from the market was regulated by the Capital Issues (Control)

Act, 1947 which was administered by the Controller of Capital Issues (CCIs) in the Ministry of Finance, Government of India. The scheme of controls under the Act required all the companies to obtain prior consent for issues of capital to the public. Pricing as well as the features of the capital structure (such as debt-equity ratios), were controlled by the Government. Similarly, the Securities Contracts (Regulation) Act, 1956 was administered by the Directorate of Stock Exchanges also in the Ministry of Finance. It empowered the Government to recognise/derecognise stock exchanges, stipulate rules and by-laws for their functioning, compel listing of securities by public companies etc. Such a system of regulation and control was fragmented and inadequate in the context of liberalisation wave sweeping across the world. Urgent measures were needed to relax controls and modernise the functioning of capital market.

2.2 Capital Market Reforms since 1991

The Indian equity market has witnessed a series of reforms since the early 1990s. The reforms have been implemented in a gradual and sequentia manner, based on international best practices and modified to suit the needs of the country. The reform measures were aimed at the following:

1. Creating growth-enabling institutions.
2. Boosting competitive conditions in the equity market through improved price discovery mechanism.
3. Putting in place an appropriate regulatory framework.
4. Reducing the transaction costs.
5. Reducing information asymmetry, thereby boosting the investor confidence.

These measures were expected to increase the role of the equity market in resource mobilisation by enhancing the access of corporate sector to large resources through a variety of marketable securities. Institutional development was at the core of the reform process.

Reforms in the capital market have had a multi-dimensional impact. The significance of the capital market has improved in providing a mechanism for allocation of resources as is reflected in increase in its share in the sources of finance for the corporates. Various indicators such as reduced volatility are pointers in the direction of increase in the safety of the market. The safety of the market has also been considerably enhanced by adoption of risk management practices and the setting up of settlement guarantee funds and investor protection funds.

The integrity and transparency of the market has also gone up with the wider availability of information regarding the performance of corporates. The trading and settlement framework in the Indian stock exchanges now compares favourably with the best international practices. Liquidity in the market has improved considerably.

2.3 Introduction of Free Pricing

Raising of capital from the securities market before 1992 was regulated under the Capital Issues (Control) Act, 1947. Firms were required to obtain approval from the Controller of Capital Issues (CCI) for raising resources in the market. New companies were allowed to issue shares only at par. Only the existing companies with substantial reserves could issue shares at a premium, which was based on some prescribed formula. In 1992, the Capital Issues (Control) Act, 1947 was repealed and with this ended all controls related to raising of resources from the market. Since then the issuers of securities can raise capital from the market without requiring any consent from any authority, either for making the issue or for pricing it. Restrictions on rights and bonus issues have also been removed. New as well as established companies are now able to price their issues according to their assessment of market conditions.

However, issuers of capital are required to meet the guidelines of SEBI on disclosure and investor protection. Companies issuing capital are required to make sufficient disclosures, including justification of the issue price and also material disclosure about the risk factors in their offer prospectus. These guidelines have served as an important measure for protecting the interest of investors and promoting the development of primary market along sound lines.

It may be recalled that in the early 1990s, the liberalisation of the industrial sector and free pricing of capital issues led to an increased number of companies tapping the primary capital market to mobilise resources. Several corporates charged a high premium not justified by their fundamentals. Also, several companies vanished after raising resources from the capital market. SEBI, therefore, strengthened the norms for public issues while retaining the freedom of the issuers to enter the new issues market and to freely price their issues. The disclosure standards were also strengthened for companies coming out with public issues for improving the levels of investor protection. Strict disclosure norms and entry point restrictions prescribed by SEBI made it difficult for most new companies without an established track record to access the public issues market. Whereas this helped to improve the quality of paper coming into the market, it contributed to a decline in the number of issues and the amount mobilised from the market.

2.4 Strengthening of Disclosure Norms

The central goal of securities markets is to obtain a widely-dispersed ownership and trading in securities. There is conflict of interest between the management team, which controls the firm, and the shareholders, who run the firm. Many policy efforts in recent years have been devoted towards improving incentives to managers to maximise the interests of shareholders.

Improvements in disclosure are a central tool for containing the conflicts of interest between the managers and shareholders. In order to foster improvements in disclosure, SEBI set up a system named electronic data information filing and retrieval (EDIFAR) in July 2002. This system offers a mechanism through which firms would electronically file mandatory disclosures to SEBI, and these documents would be available to individuals over the internet, with a near-zero delay. It is envisaged that in the future, disclosure would take place through company websites, exchange websites, and EDIFAR.

For strengthening the process of information flow from the listed companies, several measures have been introduced: (a) while sufficient disclosures are mandatory for the companies at the stage of public issues, the listed companies are also required under the listing agreement to make disclosures on a continued basis, (b) for ensuring quick flow of information to the public, the decision pertaining to dividend, bonus and right announcements or any material event are now required to be disclosed to the public within 15 minutes of the conclusion of the board meeting in which the disclosures are taken, and (c) accounting practices were streamlined with norms introduced for segment reporting, related to party transactions and consolidated balance sheets.

There is a substantial scale of securities issuance taking place through the private placement route. The private placement route has become a mechanism where securities can be placed with a few wholesale buyers of securities, without incurring the overheads of the public issue. SEBI is working on devising clear institutional mechanisms through which some public disclosure is made about these issues, while preserving the rights of issuers to not use the public issue route if it is considered to involve excessive overhead costs.

Without seeking to control the freedom of the issuers to enter the market and freely price their issues, the norms for public issues were made stringent in April 1996 to prevent fraudulent companies from accessing the market. Issuers of capital are now required to disclose information on various aspects such as track record of profitability, risk factors etc. As a result, there has been an improvement in the standards of disclosure in the offer documents for the public and rights issues and easier accessibility of information to the investors. The improvement in disclosure standards has enhanced transparency, thereby improving the level of investor protection.

2.5 Transparency and Efficiency

The National Stock Exchange (NSE) introduced screen-based trading at its inception in 1992 which was followed by other stock exchanges. Screen-based trading makes online, electronic, anonymous and order-driven transactions possible. It is a transparent system which provides equal access to all investors, irrespective of their geographical locations.

The move to an electronic trading system has resulted in transparency in trades, better price discovery and lower transaction costs. The efficiency of the market has improved through faster execution of trades. The operational efficiency of the stock market has also been strengthened through improvements in the clearing and settlement practices and the risk management process. Almost the entire delivery of securities now takes place in dematerialised form. Over the past few years or so, there has been no instance of postponement or clubbing of settlements at two main stock exchanges (BSE and NSE) despite defaults by brokers. The cases of bad deliveries are close to nil. Insider trading has been made a criminal offence. Non-transparent products like *badla* have been banned.

The setting up of trade/settlement guarantee funds in most of the exchanges has considerably reduced settlement risks for investors. Corporate governance practices and disclosure norms have led to transparency in information flows, which in turn have improved the price discovery process.

In order to bring greater transparency to the debt market, and to move away from bilateral negotiations towards anonymous order-matching, trading in government bonds began on stock exchanges on January 16, 2003. This has involved exploiting the identical process flow used for trading in equities. Trade takes place by anonymous order matching for all orders across the country, risk management is done by the clearing corporation, and settlement takes place at the depository. Under this system, government bonds appear in the depository statement of an investor alongside corporate equities and bonds. This system has several strengths.

1. Anonymous trading avoids the supervisory and regulatory difficulties of the telephone market, where counterparties are aware of identities and can engage in trades at off-market prices.
2. This market design offers symmetric market access from locations all over India and over the internet, as opposed to the telephone market, which favours entities in south Mumbai.
3. It exploits information technology to guarantees that orders are matched against the best price available in the country. This is in contrast with the telephone market, where traders can search for counterparties, but are not sure of having found the best counterparty.
4. It is fully transparent in that orders and trades are visible in real time. This is in contrast with the telephone market, where orders are not visible, and the transparency of trades is limited and delayed.
5. It exploits the information technology of the depositories of the equity market (NSDL and CDSL), which have the full range of functionality required for investors such as a wide network of IT-enabled depository participants, internet access, strong computer security, access to data about the beneficial owner down to the end-investor.

Issuers also have the option of raising resources through fixed price mechanism or the book building process. [1] Book building was introduced to improve the transparency in pricing of the scrips and determine proper market price for shares.

2.6 Shortening of Settlement Cycle

Capital, unlike labour, is perpetually recycled, and the shorter the cycle, the more efficient is the use of such capital.

Following the enactment of the Depository Act, 1996, two depositories were set up: Central Depository Services Ltd. (CDSL) and National Securities Depository Limited (NSDL). The CDSL and NSDL have been successful in the dematerialisation of securities almost to the full extent. Presently, the transfer of ownership is mostly done through book-entry form. This has greatly improved the speed, accuracy and security of the settlement system. Prior to these arrangements, the settlement cycle was as high as 14 days for specified scrips and 30 days for others. The settlement risk was very high because of unforeseen happenings between the transaction and the settlement. To begin with, the settlement cycle was reduced to a week. Thereafter, rolling settlement was introduced on a T+5 basis in July 2001. From December 2001, all scrips which had established connectivity with the above-mentioned Depositories were moved to rolling settlement. The settlement cycle was further reduced to T+3 in April 2002 and to T+2 in April 2003.

2.7 Growth of Service Providers

Besides strengthening the institutional design of the markets, the reforms have also brought about an increase in the number of service providers who add value to the market. The most significant development in this respect has been the setting up of credit rating agencies. By assigning ratings to debt instruments and by continuous monitoring and dissemination of the ratings, they help in improving the quality of information. At present, seven credit rating agencies are operating in India. Besides, two other service providers, *viz.* registrars to issue and share transfer agents, have also grown in number, which help in spreading the services easily and at competitive prices.

Endnote

1. Book-building is a process by which demand for the securities proposed to be issued is built-up and the price for securities is assessed for determination of the quantum of such securities to be issued.

3

Depository System, Dematerialisation (Demat) and Rematerialisation (Remat)

3.1 Depository System

Shares are traditionally held in physical (paper) form. This method has weaknesses like loss/theft of certificates, forged/fake certificates, cumbersome and time consuming procedure for transfer of shares etc. To eliminate these weaknesses, a new system called depository system has been established. A depository is a system which holds shares of an investor in the form of electronic accounts in the same way a bank holds money of a depositor in a savings account.

A depository holds securities in dematerialised form. It maintains ownership records of securities in a book entry form and also effects transfer of ownership through book entry.

Depository system provides the following advantages to an investor:

1. Shares cannot be lost, stolen or mutilated.
2. An investor never needs to doubt the genuineness of his shares i.e. whether they are forged or fake.
3. Share transactions like transfer, transmission etc. can be effected immediately.
4. Transaction costs are usually lower than on the physical segment.
5. There is no risk of bad delivery.
6. Bonus/rights shares allotted to an investor will be immediately credited to his account.
7. An investor receives the statement of accounts of his transactions/holdings periodically.

While the investors have a right to hold securities in either physical or demat form, SEBI has introduced some degree of compulsion in trading and settlement of securities in demat form. SEBI has mandated compulsory trading and settlement of securities in select securities in dematerialised form. This was initially introduced for institutional investors and was later extended to all investors.

3.2 National Securities Depository Limited (NSDL)

It was created in 1995. Based in Mumbai, it was the first central securities depository in India. Promoted by institutions of national stature responsible for the economic development of India, it has established a national infrastructure of international standards that handles most of the securities held and settled in dematerialised form in the Indian capital market.

Although India had a vibrant capital market which is more than a century old, the paper-based settlement of trades caused substantial problems such as bad delivery and delayed transfer of title. The enactment of Depositories Act in August 1996 paved the way for establishment of NSDL, the first depository in India. It went on to establish infrastructure based on international standards.

NSDL has the objective of ensuring the safety and soundness of Indian marketplaces by developing settlement solutions that increase efficiency, minimise risk and reduce costs. NSDL plays a quiet but central role in developing products and services that will continue to nurture the growing needs of the financial services industry.

In the depository system, securities are held in depository accounts, which are similar to holding funds in bank accounts. Transfer of ownership of securities is done through simple account transfers. This method does away with all the risks and hassles normally associated with paperwork. Consequently, the cost of transacting in a depository environment is considerably lower as compared to transacting in certificates.

NSDL is promoted by Industrial Development Bank of India Limited (IDBI)—the largest development bank of India, Unit Trust of India (UTI)—the largest mutual fund in India and National Stock Exchange of India Limited (NSE)—the largest stock exchange in India. Some of the prominent banks in the country have taken a stake in NSDL.

3.3 National Securities Clearing Corporation Ltd (NSCCL)

NSCCL, a wholly-owned subsidiary of NSE, was incorporated in August 1995 and commenced operating as a clearing corporation in April 1996. Clearing and settlement operations of the NSE are managed by NSCCL. It was the first clearing corporation to provide novation/settlement guarantee that revolutionised the entire concept of settlement system in India. It was set up to: (a) bring and sustain confidence in clearing and settlement of securities, (b) promote and maintain short and consistent settlement cycles, (c) provide counterparty risk guarantee, and (d) operate a tight risk containment system.

The settlements of trade in the equities market (both cash and derivative segments) are settled in the BSE by clearing house called BOISL which is a company jointly promoted by BSE (49 percent) and Bank of India (51 percent). BOISL, *inter alia*, handles some of the settlement-related activities of BSE as per instructions and directions of BSE. Responsibility of the clearing house is to handle such settlement activities including co-ordination with the market participants, viz. depositories, clearing banks etc.

However, the overall responsibility of settlement and risk management functions, viz. collection of margins, collateral management etc. pertaining to transactions done on BSE Online Trading (BOLT) System lies with the BSE.

NSCCL undertakes clearing of transactions executed on the National Stock Exchange for Automated Trading (NEAT) system of NSE. It carries out clearing and settlement functions as per the settlement cycles of different sub-segments in the equities segment. The reforms in the securities settlement systems have resulted in following benefits:

1. Reduction and mitigation of systemic, structural and operational risks.

2. Increase speed of transaction, execution and settlement of trade and quicker settlement of transactions with finality.
3. Safety of the settlement process.
4. Reduction of transaction costs and, thereby, making market more efficient and transparent for investors and participants.

3.4 Dematerialisation (Demat)

The concept of demat was introduced in Indian capital market in 1996 with the setting up of NSDL. Demat is the process by which the physical certificates of an investor are converted to an equivalent number of securities in electronic form and credited in the investor's account with his depository participant (DP).

When an investor decides to have his shares in electronic form, he should approach a depository participant (DP)—who is an agent of the depository—and open an account. He should then request for the dematerialisation of certificates by filling up a dematerialisation request form (DRF), which is available with the DP and submitting the same along with the physical certificates.

The investor has to ensure that before the certificates are handed over to the DP for demat, they are defaced by marking *surrendered for dematerialisation* on the face of the certificates. Before defacing the share certificate, the investor must ensure that it is available for dematerialisation. The investor must therefore check with his depository participant (DP) whether the ISIN (code number for the security in a depository system) has been activated and made available for dematerialisation by the depository. If yes, then the investor may deface the share certificate. Only those certificates can be dematerialised that are already registered in the investor's name and are in the list of securities admitted for dematerialization by National Securities Depository Limited (NSDL).

His DP will arrange to get them sent to and verified by the company, and on confirmation credit his account with an equivalent number of shares. This process is known as dematerialisation (demat). An investor can always reverse this process if he so desires and get his shares reconverted into paper format. This process is known as rematerialisation.

3.4.1 Benefits of Demat: These are the following:

1. Elimination of bad deliveries.
2. Elimination of all risks associated with physical certification.
3. No stamp duty.
4. Immediate transfer and registration of securities.
5. Faster settlement cycle.
6. Faster disbursement of rights, bonus etc.
7. Reduction in brokerage by many brokers for trading in dematerialised securities.
8. Reduction in handling of huge volumes of paper and postal delays.
9. Periodic status report.
10. Elimination of problems relating to change of address of investor, transmission etc.
11. Elimination of problems related to selling securities on behalf of a minor.
12. Ease in portfolio monitoring.

3.5 Rematerialisation (Remat)

If the investor wishes to get back his securities in physical form, all he has to do is to request his DP for rematerialisation of the same. Rematerialisation is the term used for converting electronic holdings back into certificates. An investor's DP will forward his request to NSDL, after verifying that he has the necessary balance. NSDL in turn will intimate the registrar who will print the certificates and dispatch the same to the investor.

4

Traditional Instruments of Capital Market

The maturity and sophistication of financial system depends upon the prevalence of a variety of financial instruments to suit the varied investment requirements of heterogeneous investors so as to enable it to mobilize savings from as wide section of the investing public as possible. Since early 1990s, the Indian financial system has witnessed tremendous growth in financial product innovation by corporates as well as financial institutions.

Capital market instruments fall into two broad groups: (i) direct instruments, and (ii) derivates instruments (discussed in the next chapter). Direct instruments include the following:

1. Ordinary (or equity) shares.
2. Preference shares.
3. Debentures.
4. Bonds.

While the ordinary and preference shares represent ownership instruments, debentures and innovating debt instruments are creditorship securities.

4.1 Ordinary Shares

Ordinary shares represent ownership capital and their owners—ordinary shareholders—share the reward and risk associated with ownership of corporate enterprises. They are called ordinary shares in contrast with preference shares which carry certain prior rights with regard to income and redemption.

There are certain concepts associated with ordinary shares. Authorised equity represents the maximum amount that a company can raise from the ordinary shareholders. It can be changed in the prescribed manner. The portion of the authorized capital offered by the company to investors is the issued capital. Subscribed share capital is that part of the issued capital which has been subscribed by the investors. The actual amount paid by the shareholders is the paid-up capital. The issued, subscribed and paid-up capitals are generally the same.

Ordinary shares typically have a face value in terms of the price of each share, the most popular denomination being ₹ 10. However, companies are permitted to issue such shares without a face value. The price at which the ordinary shares are issued is the issue price. The issue price for new companies is generally equal to the face value. It may be higher for existing companies, the difference being the share premium. The book value of ordinary shares refers to the paid-up capital plus reserves and surplus (net worth) divided by the number of outstanding shares. The price at which ordinary shares are traded in the stock market is their market value.

Ordinary shares have some special features in terms of the rights and claims of their holders: (a) residual claim to income/assets, (b) right to control, (c) pre-emptive rights, and (d) limited liability.

Ordinary shareholders have a residual claim to the income of the company. They are entitled to the remaining income of the company after all outside claims are met. The amount actually received by the shareholders in the form of dividend depends on the decision of the board of directors. The directors have the right to decide what portion of the earning will be distributed to the shareholders as cash dividend and what portion will be ploughed back as retained earnings, which the shareholders may receive later in the form of capital appreciation/bonus shares.

The ordinary shareholders' claim in the assets of the company is also residual in that their claim would rank after the claims of the creditors and preference shareholders in the event of liquidation. If the liquidation value of assets is insufficient, their claims may remain unpaid.

As owners of the company, ordinary shareholders have the right to control the operations of, participate in the management of, the company. Their control is, however, indirect. The major policies/decisions are approved by the board of directors and the board-appointed management carries out the day-to-day operations. The shareholders have the legal right/power to elect the board of directors as well as vote on every resolution placed in various meetings of the company.

The ordinary shareholders exercise their right to control the company through voting in the meetings of the company. According to the most commonly used system of voting in India, namely majority rule voting, each share carries one vote. As a result, shareholders/groups holding more than 50 percent of the outstanding equity shares are able to elect all the directors of their choice.

The ordinary shareholders of a company enjoy pre-emptive rights in the sense that they have a legal right to be offered, by the company, the first opportunity to purchase additional issues of equity capital in proportion to their existing holdings.

Although ordinary shareholders share the ownership risk, their liability is limited to the extent of their investment in the share capital of the company.

4.2 Preference Shares

Preference shares are a unique type of long-term capital market instruments in that they combine some of the features of ordinary shares as well as some features of debentures.

1. As a hybrid form of financial instrument, they are similar to debentures insofar as they carry a fixed rate of dividend.
2. They rank higher than ordinary shares as claimants to the income/assets of the company.
3. Generally, preference shareholders do not have voting rights.
4. They do not have a share in residual earnings/assets.
5. Dividend on preference shares is paid out of divisible/after tax profit.
6. Payment of preference dividend depends on the discretion of the management, i.e. it is not an obligatory payment and non-payment does not force insolvency/liquidation.

7. Irredeemable types of preference shares have no fixed maturity date.

Preference shares have a prior claim over ordinary shares both on the income and assets of the company. In other words, preference dividend must be paid in full before payment of any dividend on ordinary shares. In the event of liquidation, the whole of preference share capital must be paid before anything is paid to the ordinary shareholders. Thus, preference shares stand midway between debentures and ordinary shares as regards claims on the income and assets of the company. Stated in terms of risk perspective, preference shares are less risky than ordinary shares but more risky than debentures.

4.3 Debentures

Debentures represent creditorship securities and debentures holders are long-term creditors of the company. As a secured instrument, it is a promise to pay interest and repay principal at stipulated times.

The payment of interest and repayment of principal is a contractual obligation enforceable by law. Failure/default leads to bankruptcy of the company. The claim of debenture holders on income and assets ranks paripassu with other secured debt and higher than that of shareholders—preference as well as ordinary shares.

Convertible debentures give the holders the right (option) to convert them into equity shares on certain terms. They are entitled to a fixed income till the conversion option is exercised and share the benefits associated with equity shares after the conversion.

4.4 Types of Orders

In the stock market, when prices of the well-traded securities are quoted, full prices are seldom indicated. The various kinds of order given by various traders are explained below.

4.4.1 Market Order: Market order is the most common type of order and simply involves an instruction to buy or sell at the prevailing price in the market. It represents the best price one can get at a point of time. Small orders can be conveniently executed at the market rate but if the size of the order is larger than the volume which is currently available in the dealing pit, then executions might not all be at the same price because the dealer would have to bid up or offer down until desired volumes are secured. Thus, large orders *at market* have a tendency to move against those who give them. No wonder then that large orders may be placed by market participants who wish to move the market in a particular direction.

4.4.2 Limit Order: A limit order is an order to buy or sell at a specified price, or a price better than that. Thus, a limit order is exemplified when a client may give a broker a price limit above which he should not buy or below which he should not sell. Also, there is a time limit for which it may be given. This kind of an order puts more responsibility on the dealer since he has to be aware of his limits orders once the limit is reached. A limit order kind of order is feasible when it is considered that there is sufficient market force in the opposite direction at current prices. This has the advantage that it is far less likely to push prices in an adverse direction.

4.4.3 Stop-Loss Order: A stop-loss order is aimed at closing out positions when a particular price level is traded. It is this kind of an order when a client orders his broker to sell a share or some other security, if its market price falls to a certain level below the current price. Thus, once the specified price is reached or penetrated, the order becomes the market order. Stop-loss orders are a good means of protecting profits or limiting losses while waiting for the market to recover.

4.4.4 Stop-Limit Order: A stop-limit order is said to be placed when, for example, a client can place a stop order at a particular level with a limit beyond which the market would cease to be chased.

4.4.5 Fill or Kill Order: This is an order to a broker to buy or sell a security or derivative immediately. If the order is not executed at once, it is treated as withdrawn. This type of an order is often used by a party wishing to take out a large bid/offer but, in case of a failure, it does not wish to be viewed as a possible large counter party in the market.

4.4.6 Market if Touched (MIT): It is a limit order which automatically becomes a market order once a predetermined price is reached.

4.4.7 Good Till Cancelled (GTC): This is a client's order to buy or sell, usually at a specified price, which remains valid until its execution or cancellation.

4.4.8 Day Order or Good for the Day: As the name implies, this means the limits or stop order would lapse at the end of the day (of dealing) if it has not been executed during the day.

4.5 Bonds

4.5.1 What is a Bond? A bond is a fixed income investment in which an investor loans money to an entity which borrows the funds for a defined period of time at a variable or fixed interest rate. Bonds are used by companies, municipalities, states and sovereign governments to raise money and finance a variety of projects and activities. Owners of bonds are creditors of the issuer.

Bonds are commonly referred to as fixed-income securities and are one of the three main generic asset classes, along with stocks (equities) and cash equivalents. Many corporate and government bonds are publicly traded on exchanges, while others are traded only over-the-counter (OTC).

When companies or other entities need to raise money to finance new projects, maintain ongoing operations, or refinance existing debts, they may issue bonds directly to investors instead of obtaining loans from a bank. The indebted entity (issuer) issues a bond that contractually states the interest rate that will be paid and the time at which the loaned funds (bond principal) must be returned (maturity date). The interest rate, called the coupon rate or payment, is the return that bondholders earn for loaning their funds to the issuer.

The issuance price of a bond is usually ₹ 1,000 or ₹ 10,000 face value per individual bond. The actual market price of a bond depends on a number of factors including the credit quality of the issuer, the length of time until expiration, and the coupon rate compared to the general interest rate environment at the time.

4.5.2 Bond Prices Move Inversely with Interest Rates: Because fixed-rate bonds pay the same percentage of its face value over time, the market price of the bond will fluctuate as that percentage becomes desirable or undesirable given prevailing interest rates at a given moment in time. For example, if a ₹ 1,000 bond is issued at interest rate of 10 percent—when prevailing interest rates is also 10 percent—the bondholder will be credited ₹ 100 in interest income annually. The bondholder would be indifferent to purchasing the bond or saving the same money at the prevailing interest rate.

However, if interest rates in the economy drop to 8 percent, the bond will continue paying 10 percent, making it a more attractive option. Investors will purchase these bonds, bidding the price up to a premium until the effective rate of the bond equals 8 percent. On the other hand, if interest rates rise to 12 percent, the 10 percent bond rate is no longer attractive and the bond price will decrease, selling at a discount until it is effective rate is 12 percent. Because of this mechanism, bond prices move inversely with interest rates.

4.5.3 Characteristics of Bonds: Most bonds share some common basic characteristics including the following:

1. **Issue Price:** It is the price at which the bond issuer originally sells the bonds.
2. **Face Value:** It is the money amount the bond will be worth at its maturity, and is also the reference amount the bond issuer uses when calculating interest payments. For example, an investor purchases a bond at a premium (₹ 1,090) and another purchases the same bond at a discount (₹ 980). When the bond matures, both investors will receive ₹ 1,000 face value of the bond.
3. **Coupon Rate:** It is the rate of interest the bond issuer will

pay on the face value of the bond, expressed as a percentage. For example, a 10 percent coupon rate means that bondholders will receive 10 percent (₹ 100) of the face value (₹ 1,000) every year.

4. **Coupon Dates:** These are the dates on which the bond issuer will make interest payments. Typical intervals are annual or semi-annual coupon payments.
5. **Maturity Date:** It is the date on which the bond will mature and the bond issuer will pay the bond holder the face value of the bond.

Two features of a bond—credit quality and duration—are the principal determinants of a bond's interest rate. If the issuer has a poor credit rating, the risk of default is greater and these bonds will tend to trade at a discount. In addition, bonds with a high default risk, such as junk bonds, have higher interest rates than stable bonds, such as government bonds.

Longer-dated bonds have lower liquidity and hence they command a higher interest rate.

4.5.4 Varieties of Bonds: These are as under:

- **Zero-coupon Bonds:** These bonds do not pay out regular interest payments, and instead are issued at a discount and their market price eventually converges to face value upon maturity. The discount a zero-coupon bond sells for will be equivalent to the yield of a similar coupon bond.
- **Convertible Bonds:** These are debt instruments with an embedded call option that allows bondholders to convert their debt into stock (equity) at some point if the share price rises to a sufficiently high level to make such a conversion attractive.
- **Callable Bonds:** It means the issuer can call back the bonds from debt holders if interest rates drop sufficiently. These bonds typically trade at a premium to non-callable debt due to the risk of being called away and also due to their relative scarcity in the bond market.

5

Innovative Financial Instruments (Derivatives)

5.1 Emergence of Complex Financial Products

In recent years, complex financial products such as asset-backed securities, derivatives, credit-default swaps (CDSs) and collateralised debt obligations (CDOs) have proliferated in developed countries. These products have become highly popular with banks and financial institutions as they allow them to hedge their risks and manage their regulatory and economic capital more efficiently.

Although various structured products have enabled the transfer of risks and enhanced the liquidity of instruments, the recent turmoil in the US sub-prime mortgage market and related developments connected with complex derivatives have also brought to the fore the risks posed by these instruments.

The emergence of the market for derivative products, most notably forwards, futures and options, can be traced back to the willingness of risk-averse economic agents to guard themselves against uncertainties arising out of fluctuations in asset prices. By their very nature, the financial markets are marked by a very high degree of volatility. Through the use of derivative products, it is possible to partially or fully transfer price risks by locking-in asset prices. As instruments of risk management, derivatives generally do not influence the fluctuations in the underlying asset prices. However, by locking-in asset prices, derivative products minimize the impact of fluctuations in asset prices on the profitability and cash flow situation of risk-averse investors.

Derivative products initially emerged as hedging devices against fluctuations in commodity prices and commodity-linked derivatives remained the sole form of such products for a long time. The financial derivatives came into spotlight in post-1970 period due to growing instability in the financial markets. However, since their emergence, financial derivatives have become very popular and by 1990s, they accounted for about two-thirds of total transactions in derivative products. In recent years, the market for financial derivatives has grown tremendously both in terms of variety of instruments available, their complexity and also turnover.

In India also financial products such as mortgage-backed securities (MBS) and asset-backed securities (ABS) are in existence. Besides the securitised products, the Indian forex and rupee derivative markets have also developed significantly over the years.

In respect of forex derivatives involving rupee, residents have access to foreign exchange forward contracts, foreign currency-rupee swap instruments and currency options—both cross currency and foreign currency-rupee. As stated in the Annual Policy Statement for the year 2008-09, the Reserve Bank of India (RBI) announced the introduction of currency futures in the eligible exchanges for which the broad framework was announced in August 2008. In future, some more innovative and complex products might emerge. These products may pose several regulatory and supervisory challenges.

5.2 Meaning of Derivatives

Derivative in mathematics means a variable derived from another variable. The term *derivative* indicates that it has no independent value, i.e. its value is entirely *derived* from the value of the underlying asset. The underlying asset can be security, commodity, bullion, currency, live stock or anything else. In other words, derivative means a forward, future, option or any other hybrid contract of pre-determined fixed duration, linked for the purpose of contract fulfilment to the value of a specified real or financial asset of an index of securities. Similarly, in the financial sense, a derivative is a financial product, which has been derived from a market for another product. Without the underlying product, derivatives do not have any independent existence in the market.

Derivative instruments are defined by the Indian Securities Contracts (Regulation) Act, 1956 to include: (i) a security derived from a debt instrument, share, secured/unsecured loan, risk instrument or contract for differences, or any other form of security, and (ii) a contract that derives its value from the prices/index of prices of underlying securities.

In other words, derivatives are financial instruments whose value depends upon the value of an underlying. Since their value is essentially derived out of an underlying, they are financial abstractions whose value is derived mathematically from the changes in the value of the underlying.

International Monetary Fund (IMF) defines derivatives as, "financial instruments that are linked to a specific financial instrument or indicator or commodity and through which specific financial risks can be traded in financial markets in their own right. The value of a financial derivative derives from the price of an underlying item, such as an asset or index. Unlike debt securities, no principal is advanced to be repaid and no investment income accrues".

Derivatives have come into being because of the existence of risks in business. Thus, derivatives are means of managing risks. The parties managing risks in the market are known as *hedgers*. Some people/organizations are in the business of taking risks to earn profits. Such entities represent the *speculators*. The third players in the market, known as the *arbitragers,* take advantage of the market mistakes.

In recent years, derivatives have become increasingly important in the field of finance. While futures and options are now actively traded on many exchanges, forward contracts are popular on the over-the-counter (OTC) market.

5.3 Reasons for the Popularity of Derivatives

Financial derivatives have become popular due to the following reasons:

1. Increased volatility in asset prices in financial markets.

2. Increased integration of national financial markets with the international markets.
3. Marked improvement in communication facilities and sharp decline in their costs.
4. Development of more sophisticated risk management tools, providing economic agents a wider choice of risk management strategies.
5. Innovations in the derivatives markets, which optimally combine the risks and returns over a large number of financial assets, leading to higher returns, reduced risk as well as transaction costs as compared to individual financial assets.

In the class of equity derivatives, futures and options on stock indices have gained more popularity than on individual stocks, especially among institutional investors, who are major users of index-linked derivatives. Even small investors find these useful due to high correlation of the popular indices with various portfolios and ease of use. The lower costs associated with index derivatives vis-à-vis derivative products based on individual securities is another reason for their growing use.

5.4 Variants (or Types) of Derivative Contracts

Derivative contracts have several variants. The most common variants are forwards, futures, options and swaps.

5.4.1 Forwards/Forward Contracts: A forward contract is a customised contract between two entities, where settlement takes place on a specific date in the future at today's pre-agreed price. A forward contract is an agreement to buy or sell an asset on a specified date for specified price. One of the parties to the contract assumes a long position and agrees to buy the underlying asset on a certain specified future date, for a certain specified price. The other party assumes a short position and agrees to sell the asset on the same date for the same price. Other contract details like delivery date, price and quantity are negotiated bilaterally by the parties to the contract.

Forward contracts are normally traded outside stock

exchanges. They are popular on the over the counter (OTC) market. The salient features of forward contracts are as follows:

1. They are bilateral contracts and hence exposed to counter party risk.
2. Each contract is customer designed, and, hence, is unique in terms of contract size, expiration date and the asset type and quality.
3. The contract price is generally not available in public domain.
4. On the expiration date, the contract has to be settled by delivery for the asset.
5. If a party wishes to reverse the contract, it has to compulsorily go to the same counterparty, which often results in a high price being charged.

Forward contracts are very useful in hedging and speculation. A typical hedging application may pertain to an exporter who expects to receive payment in US dollars, 2 months later. He is exposed to the risk of exchange rate fluctuations. By using the currency forward market to sell dollars forward, he can lock-on a rate today and reduce his uncertainty. Likewise, an importer who is required to make a payment in US dollars 2 months hence can reduce his exposure to exchange rate fluctuations by buying dollars forward.

5.4.2 Futures/Future Contracts: Future contracts are special types of forward contracts in the sense that the former are standardised exchange-traded contracts. Future contract markets are designed to solve the problems that exist in forward markets. A future contract is an agreement between two parties to buy or sell an asset at a certain time in future, at a certain price. However, unlike forward contracts, future contracts are standardized and stock exchange-traded. To facilitate liquidity in the future contracts, the exchange specifies certain standard features for the contract. It is a standardized contract with a standard underlying instrument, a standard quantity and quality of the underlying instrument that can be delivered, and a standard timing of such settlement. A future contract may be offset prior to maturity by entering into an equal and opposite transaction. The standardized items in a future contract are the following:

1. Quantity of the underlying.
2. Quality of the underlying.
3. Date/month of delivery.
4. Units of price quotation and minimum price change.
5. Location of settlement.

5.4.3 Options: Options are fundamentally different from forward and future contracts. An option gives the holder of the option the right to do something. The holder does not have to necessarily exercise this right. In contrast, in a forward or future contract, the two parties commit themselves to doing something. Whereas it costs nothing (except margin requirements) to enter into a future contract, the purchase of an option requires an up front payment.

Options are of two types: calls options and put options. Calls options give the buyer the right but not the obligation to buy a given quantity of the underlying asset, at a given price on or before a given future date. Put options give the buyer the right, but not the obligation to sell a given quantity of the underlying asset at a given price on or before a given date.

A. Warrants: Options generally have lives of up to 1 year, the majority of options traded on options exchanges having maximum maturity of 9 months. Longer-dated options are called *warrants* and are generally traded over-the-counter.

B. LEAPS: The acronym LEAPS means Long-term Equity Anticipation Securities. These are options having a maturity of up to 3 years.

C. Baskets: Basket options are options on portfolios of underlying assets. The underlying asset is usually a moving average or a basket of assets. Equity index options are a form of basket options.

5.4.4 Swaps: Swaps are private agreements between two parties to exchange cash flows in the future according to a pre-arranged formula. They can be regarded as portfolios of forward contracts. Following are the two commonly used swaps:

A. Interest Rate Swaps: These entail swapping of only the interest-related cash flows between the parties in the same currency.

B. Currency Swaps: These entail swapping of both principal and interest between the parties, with the cash flows in one direction being in a different currency than those in the opposite direction.

5.4.5 Swaptions: Swaptions are options to buy or sell a swap that will become operative at the expiry of the options. Thus, swaption is an option on a forward swap. Rather than have call options and put options, the swaptions market has receiver swaptions and payer swaptions.

5.5 Participants in the Derivatives Market

The following three broad categories of participants, viz. hedgers, speculators, and arbitrageurs trade in the derivatives market.

5.5.1 Hedgers: Hedgers face risk associated with the price of an asset. They use future or option markets to reduce or eliminate this risk. In other words, hedgers are those who wish to protect their existing exposures and essentially are safety-driven.

5.5.2 Speculators: They bet on future movements in the price of an asset. Future and option contracts can give them an extra leverage; that is, they can increase both the potential gains and potential losses in a speculative venture. Speculators are willing risk takers who are expectation-driven.

5.5.3 Arbitrageurs: They are in business to take advantage of a discrepancy between prices in two different markets. If, for example, they see the futures price of an asset getting out of line with the cash price, they will take offsetting positions in the two markets to lock-in a profit. Arbitragers are traders and market-makers who deal in buying and selling derivatives contracts hoping to profit from price-differentials between different markets. A market maker is one who provides two-way quotes for a given product and thereby runs a position in that product.

5.6 Economic Role of Derivatives

Derivative markets perform three essential economic functions:

1. Risk management.
2. Price discovery.
3. Transactional efficiency.

The first function refers to the ability of traders to offset financial risks through derivatives. The principal benefit of the derivatives market is that it provides the opportunity for risk management through hedging. [1] Derivatives are innovations in risk management not in risk itself.

The second refers to the better allocation of resources in an economy that is created by the wide availability of an equilibrium price which serves as a measure of value.

The third function alludes to increased efficiency of transacting through derivatives. Derivative markets reduce the costs of trading and raising capital, thereby enhancing their risk management and price discovery functions.

Derivatives have played a major role in the development of financial markets and their integration across several economies, especially in developed countries. Derivatives serve to achieve a more complete financial system because previously fixed combinations of the risk properties of loans and financial assets can be bundled and unbundled into new synthetic assets.

For instance, structured products or synthetic derivatives could be created by adding elementary assets or underlying assets such as bonds, equities and borrowing and lending instruments with a combination of derivative products such as put and call options.

Repackaging risk properties in this way can provide a more perfect match between an investor's risk preferences and the effective risk of the portfolio or cash-flow. Derivatives allow individual risk elements of an asset to be priced and traded individually, thus ensuring an efficient price system in the asset markets.

The economic functions performed by derivatives market

can be summarised as under:

1. Derivatives market helps to increase savings and investment in the long-run. Transfer of risk enables market participants to expand their volume of activity.
2. Derivatives trading acts as a catalyst for new entrepreneurial activity. Derivatives have a history of attracting many bright, creative, well educated people with an entrepreneurial attitude.
3. Prices in an organized derivatives market reflect the perception of the market participants about the future and lead the prices of underlying to the perceived future level.
4. Prices of derivatives converge with the prices of the underlying at the expiration of the derivatives contract. In fact, derivatives help in the discovery of the future as well as current prices.
5. Derivatives market helps to transfer risks from those who have them but may not like them to those who have an appetite for them.
6. Derivatives, due to their inherent nature are linked to the underlying cash markets. With the introduction of derivatives, the underlying market witnesses higher trading volumes because of participation by more players who would not otherwise participate for lack of an arrangement to transfer risk.
7. Speculative trades shift to a more controlled environment of derivatives market. In the absence of an organized derivatives market, speculators trade in the underlying cash markets. Margining, monitoring and surveillance of the activities of various participants become extremely difficult in these kinds of mixed markets.

5.7 Derivative Instruments in India

India has introduced different equity derivatives in a phased manner. This phased approach was adopted in India with index futures being introduced in June 2000, index options in June 2001 and individual stock options in July 2001.

5.7.1 L.C. Gupta Committee on Derivatives Trading in India: Securities and Exchange Board of India (SEBI) set up a 24-member committee under the Chairmanship of L.C. Gupta on November 18, 1996 to develop appropriate regulatory framework for derivatives trading in India. The Committee submitted its report on March 17, 1998 prescribing necessary preconditions for introduction of derivatives trading in India. The committee recommended that derivatives should be declared as *securities* so that regulatory framework applicable to trading of *securities* could also govern trading of derivatives. The Committee believed that regulation should be designed to achieve specific, well-defined goals. It was inclined towards positive regulation designed to encourage healthy activity and behaviour.

SEBI also set up a group in June 1998 under the chairmanship of Professor J.R. Varma, to recommend measures for risk containment in derivatives market in India. The report, which was submitted in October 1998, worked out the operational details of margining system, methodology for charging initial margins, net worth of brokers, deposit requirements and real-time monitoring requirements.

5.7.2 Credit Derivatives: The credit market refers to the market where financial instruments that embrace credit risk are traded. In addition to traditional instruments, such as loans and advances, corporate bonds, and commercial papers the credit market now includes securitised products in which various credit risks have been pooled as well as credit derivatives whose underlying assets encompass credit risks.

In a financial system, dominated by bank intermediation, credit has traditionally been the main source of funds to various sectors in the Indian economy, and loans and advances continue to be the preferred part of asset books of banks. However, the implementation of risk management guidelines and the requirement for providing a capital charge for credit risk in the balance sheet has given banks an incentive to look for innovative methods of transferring credit risk from their books.

While simple techniques for transferring credit risk, such as financial guarantees, collateral and credit insurance have long been prevalent in the Indian banking industry, the recent innovative instruments in credit risk transfer are yet to make an impact. However, in recent years the risk management architecture of banks in India has strengthened and they are on the way to becoming Basel II compliant, providing adequate comfort level for the introduction of credit derivatives.

The Reserve Bank in its Annual Policy announced in April 2007 mentioned that as part of the gradual process of financial sector liberalization in India, it was considered appropriate to introduce credit derivatives in a calibrated manner. Furthermore, the amendment to the Reserve Bank of India Act, 1934, had provided legality to OTC (over the counter) derivative instruments, including credit derivatives.

Although derivative instruments were introduced in July 1999 in the money/foreign exchange market in the form of forward rate agreements (FRAs) [2] and interest rate swaps (IRS), [3] credit derivatives are yet to be introduced. The RBI's Annual Policy Statement 2007-08 announced the introduction of credit derivatives in India in a calibrated manner. In view of certain adverse developments in the international financial markets, especially credit markets, resulting from recent financial turmoil, it was widely felt that time is not opportune to introduce the credit derivatives in India for the present. As such, the RBI announced on June 19, 2008 its decision to keep in abeyance the issuance of the final guidelines on introduction of credit derivatives in India.

5.7.3 National Exchange for Automated Trading (NEAT-F&O): Futures and options trading system of NSE—called NEAT-F&O trading system—provides a fully automated screen-based trading for index futures and options, stock futures and options and futures on interest rate on a nationwide basis as well as an online monitoring and surveillance mechanism. It supports an order driven market and provides complete transparency of trading operations. It is similar to that of trading of equities in the cash market segment.

The software for the F&O market has been developed to facilitate efficient and transparent trading in futures and options instruments. Keeping in view the familiarity of trading members with the current capital market trading system, modifications have been introduced in the existing capital market trading system so as to make it suitable for trading futures and options.

The NEAT-F&O system supports an order driven market, wherein orders match automatically. Order matching is essentially on the basis of security, its price, time and quantity. All quantity fields are in units and price in rupees. The lot size on the futures and options market is 50 for Nifty. The exchange notifies the regular lot size and tick size for each security traded on this segment from time to time. Orders, as and when they are received, are first time stamped and then immediately processed for potential match. When any order enters the trading system, it is an active order. If it finds a match, a trade is generated. If a match is not found, then the orders are stored in different books. Orders are stored in price-time priority in various books in the following sequence: (a) best price, and (b) within price, by time priority.

To sum up, financial derivatives are of recent origin in India, barring trade-related forward contracts in the forex market. Over the counter (OTC) as well as exchange-traded derivatives have been introduced, marking an important development in the structure of financial markets in India. Forward contracts in the forex market have also been liberalised. OTC derivatives, viz. interest rate swaps (IRS) and forward rate agreements (FRAs) were introduced in July 1999. The IRS and FRA were introduced with a view to deepening the money market as also to enable banks, primary dealers and financial institutions to hedge interest rate risks.

Endnotes

1. Hedging is the process of stabilizing the value of a given portfolio by neutralizing adverse market movements.

2. The FRA is an off-balance sheet contract between two parties under which one party agrees on the start date for trade and the party that agrees, would lodge a notional deposit with the other for a specified sum of money for a specified period of time (the FRA period) at a specified rate of interest (the contract rate). The party that has agreed to make the notional deposit has, thus, sold the FRA to the other party who has bought it.
3. The IRS is a contract between two counter-parties for exchange interest payment for a specified period based on a notional principal amount. The notional principal is used to calculate interest payments, but is not exchanged. Only interest payments are exchanged.

6

Modernisation of Stock Exchanges

6.1 Stock Market

A stock (or share) market deals mainly in corporate securities. The securities are chiefly in the form of equity shares and debentures. The purpose of these securities is to raise long-term funds for companies engaged in production. The function of the stock market is two-fold: (a) to arrange for the raising of new capital (primary market function), and (b) to provide liquidity to existing securities (secondary market function).

The new capital is raised by the issue of shares and debentures. The corporate enterprises raising new capital may be new companies or existing companies planning expansion of their operations. Sometimes, existing private firms go public, i.e. become public limited companies.

The stock market helps the floatation of new issues by providing a variety of services like underwriting, distribution, and listing of the issue. Underwriting means guaranteeing the purchase of a fixed amount of new issues by the underwriter. The new issues of capital may be a public issue or a rights issue or both in certain proportions. It may be in the form of equity shares or debentures. Debentures, in turn, may be fully convertible, partly convertible, or non-convertible into shares. A public issue implies that the general public is invited to subscribe to the new issue. A rights issue is restricted for subscription by existing shareholders.

Stock market provides facilities for secondary market, i.e. transaction in existing securities. People desirous of converting their cash into securities can go to the stock exchange and buy securities with the help of brokers there. Similarly, securities can be converted into cash by selling them in the market. Transactions in the secondary market reflect the investment climate in the economy. A well-developed stock market helps to access external capital which allows financially constrained domestic firms to expand. It is argued that countries with developed stock markets tend to grow faster.

6.1.1 Limitations of Stock Market: It is argued that stock market expansion is not a necessary indication of a country's financial development and stock market development may not help in achieving quicker industrialisation and faster long-term economic growth because of following reasons:

1. Due to inherent volatility and arbitrariness of the stock market, the resulting pricing process is a poor guide to efficient investment allocation.
2. In the wake of unfavourable economic shocks, the interactions between the stock and currency markets may exacerbate macroeconomic instability and reduce long-term economic growth.
3. Stock market development is likely to undermine the financial inclusion role of existing banking systems in developing countries like India.

6.2 Trading Infrastructure in Stock Exchanges

There are 3 permanent stock exchanges in India, including the old established Bombay Stock Exchange (BSE) and the National Stock Exchange (NSE) that was set up as a model exchange to provide nation-wide services to investors. The Bombay Stock Exchange (BSE) was set up in 1875 as 'The Native Share and Stock Brokers Association'.

Equity trading is most active in the two major competing stock exchanges, viz. NSE and the BSE. Trading infrastructure in the stock exchanges is anonymous and order-driven, with all orders from market participants being matched based on strike price/time priority.

The Indian capital market is significant in terms of its degree of development, its volume of trading and of the quality of its automated trading and settlement.

The capital markets—though they have suffered from

periodic scandals and problems in the past—look much closer in quality to those of developed markets than those in the majority of emerging markets. The range and quality of available securities is evidenced by the substantial flows of foreign institutional investors.

6.3 Bombay Stock Exchange (BSE) Ltd.

BSE is a stock exchange located on Dalal Street, Mumbai. It was the 10th largest stock exchange in the world by market capitalisation as of November 2018.

Established in 1875, BSE Ltd. (formerly known as Bombay Stock Exchange Ltd.), is India's second oldest stock exchange (Oldest being the Calcutta Stock Exchange Ltd. located at Lyons Range, Kolkata) and one of India's leading exchange groups.

In August 31, 1957, the BSE became the first stock exchange to be recognized by the Indian Government under the Securities Contracts Regulation Act. In 1980 the exchange moved to the Phiroze Jeejeebhoy Towers at Dalal Street, Fort area. In 1986 it developed the BSE SENSEX index, giving the BSE a means to measure overall performance of the exchange. In 2000, the BSE used this index to open its derivatives market, trading SENSEX futures contracts. The development of SENSEX options along with equity derivatives followed in 2001 and 2002, expanding the BSE's trading platform.

BSE has facilitated the growth of the Indian corporate sector by providing it an efficient capital-raising platform. BSE is a corporatized and demutualised entity, with a broad chorholder-base which includes two leading global exchanges, Deutsche Bourse, Fuse and Singapore Exchange as strategic partners. BSE provides an efficient and transparent market for trading in equity, debt instruments, derivatives, mutual funds. It also has a platform for trading in equities of small and medium enterprises (SMEs). More than 5,000 companies are listed on BSE making it world's top most exchange in terms of listed members.

BSE is world's fifth most active exchange in terms of number of transactions handled through its electronic trading system. It was also one of the world's leading exchanges (5th largest in December 2013) for Index options trading (Source: World Federation of Exchanges).

BSE also provides a host of other services to capital market participants including risk management, clearing, settlement, market data services and education. It has a global reach with customers around the world and a nation-wide presence.

BSE systems and processes are designed to safeguard market integrity, drive the growth of the Indian capital market and stimulate innovation and competition across all market segments. BSE is the first exchange in India and second in the world to obtain an ISO 9001:2000 certification. It is also the first exchange in the country and second in the world to receive Information Security Management System Standard BS 7799-2-2002 certification for its On-Line Trading System (BOLT).

It operates one of the most respected capital market educational institutes in the country (the BSE Institute Ltd.). BSE also provides depository services through its Central Depository Services Ltd. (CDSL) arm.

BSE's popular equity index—the S&P BSE SENSEX (formerly SENSEX)—is India's most widely tracked stock market benchmark index. It is traded internationally on the EUREX as well as leading exchanges of the BRCS nations (Brazil, Russia, China and South Africa). On February 19, 2013, BSE entered into Strategic Partnership with S&P DOW JONES INDICES and the SENSEX was renamed as S&P BSE SENSEX.

Historically, an open outcry floor trading exchange, the BSE switched to an electronic trading system in 1995. This automated, screen-based trading platform is called BSE on-line trading (BOLT). BSE has also introduced the world's first centralized exchange-based internet trading system, BSEWEBx.co.in to enable investors anywhere in the world to trade on the BSE platform.

6.4 National Stock Exchange of India Ltd. (NSE)

It is located in Mumbai, India. NSE was established in the

mid-1990s as a demutualised electronic exchange. NSE provides a modern, fully automated screen-based trading system, with over two lakh trading terminals, through which investors in every nook and corner of India can trade. NSE has played a critical role in reforming the Indian securities market and in bringing unparalleled transparency, efficiency and market integrity.

Though a number of other exchanges exist, NSE and the Bombay Stock Exchange (BSE) are the two most significant stock exchanges in India, and between them are responsible for the vast majority of share transactions. NSE's flagship index, the CNX NIFTY 50, is used extensively by investors in India and around the world to take exposure to the Indian equities market.

NSE was started by a clutch of leading Indian financial institutions. It offers trading, clearing and settlement services in equity, debt and equity derivatives. It is India's largest exchange, globally in cash market trades, in currency trading and index options. NSE has diversified shareholding. There are many domestic and global institutions and companies that hold stake in the exchange.

NSC was incorporated in 1992 and recognised as a stock exchange in 1993, at a time when P.V. Narasimha Rao was the Prime Minister of India and Dr. Manmohan Singh was the Finance Minister. It was set up to bring in transparency in the markets. Promoted by leading financial institutions, essentially led by IDBI at the behest of the Government of India, it was incorporated in November 1992 as a tax-paying company. In April 1993, it was recognised as a stock exchange under the Securities Contracts (Regulation) Act, 1956. NSE commenced operations in the Wholesale Debt Market (WDM) segment in June 1994. The capital market (equities) segment of the NSE commenced operations in November 1994, while operations in the derivatives segment commenced in June 2000.

NSE changed the way the Indian markets functioned, in the early 1990s, by replacing floor-based trading with nationwide screen-based electronic trading, which took trading to the doorstep of the investor. The exchange was mainly set up to bring in transparency in the markets. Instead of trading membership being confined to a group of brokers, the NSE ensured that anyone who was qualified, experienced and met minimum financial requirements was allowed to trade.

In this context, the NSE was ahead of its times, when it separated ownership and management in the exchange under SEBI's supervision. The price information which could earlier be accessed only by a handful of people can now be seen by a client in a remote location with the same ease. The paper-based settlement has been replaced by electronic depository-based accounts and settlement of trades. A robust risk management system is in place, so that settlement guarantees could protect investors against broker defaults.

NSE was also instrumental in creating the National Securities Depository Limited (NSDL) which allows investors to securely hold and transfer their shares and bonds electronically. It also allows investors to hold and trade in as few as one share or bond. This not only makes holding financial instruments convenient, but more importantly eliminates the need for paper certificates and greatly reduces the incidents of forged or fake certificates and fraudulent transactions that had plagued the Indian stock market. NSDL's security, combined with the transparency, lower transaction prices and efficiency that the NSE offers, has greatly increased the attractiveness of the Indian stock market to domestic and international investors.

Currently, NSE has the following major segments of the capital market:

- **Equities:** Equities, indices, mutual funds, exchange traded funds, initial public offerings, security lending and borrowing scheme, and sovereign gold bond scheme.
- **Derivatives:** Equity derivatives (including Global Indices like S&P 500, Dow Jones and FTSE), currency derivatives, commodity derivatives and interest rate futures.
- **Debt:** Corporate bonds, NSE EBP, and tri-party repo.

6.4.1 Equity Derivatives: NSE commenced trading in derivatives with the launch of index futures on June 12, 2000. The futures and options segment of NSE has made a mark for itself globally. In the futures and options segment, trading in CNX Nifty Index, CNX IT Index, Bank Nifty Index, Nifty Midcap 50 index and single stock futures are available. Trading in Mini Nifty Futures and Options and Long-term Options on CNX Nifty are also available.

On August 29, 2011, NSE launched derivative contracts on the world's most followed equity indices, the S&P 500 and the Dow Jones Industrial Average. NSE is the first Indian exchange to launch global indices. This is also the first time in the world that futures contracts on the S&P 500 index were introduced and listed on an exchange outside of their home country, USA. The new contracts include futures on both the DJIA and the S&P 500, and options on the S&P 500.

On May 3, 2012, NSE launched derivative contracts (futures and options) on FTSE 100, the widely tracked index of the UK equity stock market. This was the first of its kind of an index of the UK equity stock market launched in India. FTSE 100 includes 100 largest UK listed blue chip companies.

On January 10, 2013, NSE signed a letter of intent with the Japan Exchange Group, Inc. (JPX) on preparing for the launch of CNX Nifty Index futures, a representative stock price index of India, on the Osaka Securities Exchange Co., Ltd. (OSE), a subsidiary of JPX. Moving forward, both parties will make preparations for the listing of yen-denominated CNX Nifty Index futures by March 2014. Retail and institutional investors in Japan will be able to take a view on the Indian markets in their own currency and in their own time zone. Investors will therefore not face any currency risk, because they will not have to invest in dollar denominated or rupee denominated contracts.

6.4.2 Currency Derivatives: In August 2008, currency derivatives were introduced in India by NSE with the launch of currency futures in US$ and INR. It also added currency futures in Euros, Pounds and Yen.

6.4.3 Interest Rate Futures: Interest rate futures were introduced for the first time in India by NSE on August 31, 2009, exactly one year after the launch of currency futures. NSE became the first stock exchange to get an approval for interest rate futures, as recommended by the SEBI-RBI committee.

6.4.4 Debt Market: On May 13, 2013, NSE launched India's first dedicated debt platform to provide a liquid and transparent trading platform for debt related products. The debt segment provides an opportunity to retail investors to invest in corporate bonds on a liquid and transparent exchange platform. It also helps institutions who are holders of corporate bonds. It is an ideal platform to buy and sell at optimum prices and help corporates to get adequate demand, when they are issuing the bonds.

6.4.5 Financial Literacy: NSE is keen to ensure that the people of India are empowered to take sound financial decisions and invest wisely. It has collaborated, among others, with several universities like Gokhale Institute of Politics and Economics, Pune; Bharati Vidyapeeth Deemed University, Pune; Guru Gobind Singh Indraprastha University, Delhi; Ravenshaw University of Cuttack and Punjabi University, Patiala, to offer MBA and BBA courses. NSE has also provided mock market simulation software called NSE Learn to Trade (NLT) to develop investment, trading and portfolio management skills among the students. The simulation software is very similar to the software currently being used by the market professionals and helps students to learn how to trade in the markets.

The exchange has also worked with a missionary zeal to educate investors about the opportunities in the market, the precautions they should take and their rights and obligations. In order to educate investors and help them invest wisely, NSE conducts nearly 1,500 seminars every year in the metros as well as the smallest towns of India.

NSE also conducts online examination and awards certification, under its Certification in Financial Markets (NCFM) programmes. At present, certifications are available in 46 modules, covering different sectors of financial and capital markets, both at the beginner and advanced levels. The list of various modules can be found at the official site of NSE India. In addition, since August 2009, it offers a short-term course called NSE certified capital market professional (NCCMP). The NCCMP is a 100 hour programme for over 3-4 months, conducted at the colleges, and covers theoretical and practical training in subjects related to the capital markets. NCCMP covers subjects like equity markets, debt markets, derivatives, macroeconomics, technical analysis and fundamental analysis. Successful candidates are awarded joint certification from NSE and the concerned college.

The competition between NSE and BSE is a unique one by international standards, where both exchanges are in the same city and have the same trading hours. All major stocks trade on both exchanges, so the exchanges compete for order flow, and not just listings. The rise of NSE has proved to be a powerful spur to reforms at the BSE. Months after NSE started operations, the BSE also launched electronic trading, and improved rules governing admission of corporate and foreign brokerage firms. Presently, the BSE also uses an open electronic limit order book market, using satellite communications to reach locations outside Bombay.

Associated with the NSE are the National Securities Depositary Ltd. (NSDL) and the National Securities Clearing Corporation Ltd. (NSCCL). The NSDL acts as the registrar for what are now predominantly dematerialized securities and the NSCCL as a clearing house.

The setting up of the NSE as an electronic trading platform set a benchmark of operating efficiency for other stock exchanges in the country. The establishment of NSDL in 1996 and Central Depository Services (India) Ltd. (CSDL) in 1999 has enabled paperless trading in the exchanges. This has also facilitated instantaneous electronic transfer of securities and eliminated the risks to the investors arising from bad deliveries in the market, delays in share transfer, fake and forged shares and loss of scrips. The electronic funds transfer (EFT) facility combined with dematerialisation of shares has created a conducive environment for reducing the settlement cycle in stock markets.

6.5 Demutualisation and Corporatisation of Stock Exchanges

Stock exchanges all over the world were traditionally formed as *mutual* organisations. The trading members not only provided broking services, but also owned, controlled and managed such exchanges for their mutual benefit. Demutualisation refers to the transition process of an exchange from a *mutually-owned* association to a company *owned by shareholders*. In other words, transforming the legal structure of an exchange from a mutual form to a business corporation form is referred to as demutualisation. The above, in effect means that after demutualisation, the ownership, the management and the trading rights at the exchange are segregated from one another.

In a mutual exchange, the three functions of ownership, management and trading are intervened into a single group. Here, the broker members of the exchange are both the owners and the traders on the exchange and they further manage the exchange as well. A demutualised exchange, on the other hand, has all these three functions clearly segregated, i.e. the ownership, management and trading are in separate hands.

In India, NSE was set up as a demutualised corporate body, where ownership, management and trading rights are in the hands of three different sets of groups from its inception. The Stock Exchange, Mumbai—one of the two premier exchanges in the country—has since been corporatised and demutualised and renamed as the Bombay Stock Exchange Ltd. (BSE).

Corporate governance has emerged as an important tool for

protection of shareholders. The corporate governance framework in India has evolved over a period of time since the setting up of the Kumar Mangalam Birla Committee by SEBI. India has a reasonably well-designed regulatory framework for the issuance and trading of securities, and disclosures by the issuers with strong focus on corporate governance standards.

To enhance the level of continuous disclosure by the listed companies, SEBI amended the listing agreement to incorporate segment reporting, related party disclosures, consolidated financial results and consolidated financial statements. The listing agreement between the stock exchanges and the companies has been strengthened from time to time to enhance corporate governance standards.

7

Corporate Debt Market

Sound development of various segments of the capital market is a pre-requisite for a well-functioning financial system. The equity market in India has been modernised over the years and is now comparable with the international markets. There has been a visible improvement in trading and settlement infrastructure, risk management systems and levels of transparency. These improvements have brought about a reduction in the transaction costs and led to improvement in liquidity. However, the size of the public issue segment has remained small as corporates have tended to prefer the international capital market and the private placement market. This has affected the growth of the public issues market and led to under-participation by the investors in the capital market.

The corporate bond market, in particular, has remained underdeveloped, possibly due to the absence of a reliable and liquid yield curve, long time taken for floating an issue, high cost of issuance and lack of liquidity in the secondary market. The promotion of a vibrant corporate bond market is essential for meeting the demand for long-term funds, especially for infrastructure requirements.

7.1 Significance of the Corporate Debt Market

There are many reasons why bond markets are important for an emerging economy. Prominent among these is the fact that they lead to more efficient entrepreneurship and greater value creation. When an entrepreneur takes a loan or issues bonds, all additional profit over and above the pre-fixed repayment amount accrues to the entrepreneur. So he or she is better incentivized to take sharper decisions. By having a weak bond market, this efficiency is lost. Further, this efficiency gap may well mean that there is less lending and hence less investment and entrepreneurship in the economy than is feasible.

In any country, companies face different types of financing choices at different stages of development. Reflecting the varied supplies of different types of capital and their costs, regulatory policies and financial innovations, the financing patterns of firms vary geographically and temporally. While developed countries rely more on market-based sources of finance, the developing countries rely more on bank-based sources. The development of a corporate bond market, for direct financing of the capital requirements of corporates by investors assumes paramount importance, particularly in a liberalised financial system.

Corporate debt market provides an alternative means of long-term resources to corporates—alternative to financing by banks and financial institutions. The size and growth of private corporate debt market depends upon several factors, including financing patterns of companies. Among market-based sources of financing, while the equity markets have been largely developed, the corporate bond markets in most developing countries have remained relatively underdeveloped. This has been the result of dominance of the banking system combined with the weaknesses in market infrastructure and inherent complexities.

However, credit squeeze following the Asian financial crisis in the mid-1990s drew attention of policy makers to the importance of multiple financing channels in an economy. Alternative sources of finance, apart from banks, need to be actively developed to support higher levels of investment and economic growth. The development of corporate debt market has, therefore, become the prime concern of regulators in developing countries.

From the perspective of developing countries, a liquid corporate bond market can play a critical role in supporting economic development in the following ways:

1. It supplements the banking system to meet the requirements

of the corporate sector for long-term capital investment and asset creation.

2. It provides a stable source of finance when the equity market is volatile.
3. With the decline in the role of specialised financial institutions, there is an increasing realisation of the need for a well-developed corporate debt market as an alternative source of finance.
4. Corporate bond markets can also help firms reduce their overall cost of capital by allowing them to tailor their asset and liability profiles to reduce the risk of maturity and currency mismatches.
5. Corporate bond market is important for nurturing a credit culture and market discipline.
6. The existence of a well-functioning bond market can lead to the efficient pricing of credit risk as expectations of all bond market participants are incorporated into bond prices.

Apart from providing a channel for financing investments, the corporate bond markets also contribute towards portfolio diversification for holders of long-term funds. Effective asset management requires a balance of asset alternatives. In view of the underdeveloped state of the corporate bond markets, there would be an overweight position in government securities and even equities. The existence of a well-functioning corporate bond market widens the array of asset choices for long-term investors such as pension funds and insurance companies and allows them to better manage the maturity structure of their balance sheets.

7.2 Developments in the Corporate Debt Market

India is now one of the fastest growing economies in the world and is endeavouring to step up the growth rate. Limited availability of adequate long-term resources could adversely affect India's infrastructure development. Infrastructure financing requirements are large and could not be expected to be met by the banking sector alone. Banks already appear to have significant exposure to long-term funds. They may, therefore, not be in a position to fund long-term projects in future to the extent they have been able to do in recent years.

Inadequate long-term resources could, therefore, act as a constraint on India's future growth prospects. In the absence of a well-functioning debt market, even large corporates fund their requirements from the banking system, limiting the availability of bank funds for small and medium enterprises and other sectors. This also raises the cost of borrowings for them. Thus, development of the capital market, in general, and the debt market, in particular, is crucial from the point of view of reducing corporate sector's reliance on the banking system so as to enable it to focus more on lending to small and medium enterprises, and agriculture and allied activities.

Corporates in India have traditionally relied heavily on borrowings from banks and financial institutions (FIs) to finance their investments. Equity financing has also been used, but largely during periods of surging equity prices. However, bond issuances by companies have remained limited in size and scope. Given the huge funding requirements, especially for long-term infrastructure projects, the corporate debt market has a crucial role to play and needs to be nurtured.

In India, banks and FIs have traditionally been the most important external sources of finance for the corporate sector. The second half of the 1980s saw some activity in primary bond issuances, but these were largely by the public sector undertakings (PSUs). The corporates relied more on banks for meeting short-term working capital requirements and DFIs for financing long-term investment. However, in view of the declining role of DFIs in recent years, a gap has appeared for long-term finance. Commercial banks have managed to fill this gap, but only to an extent as there are asset-liability mismatch issues for banks in providing longer-maturity credit.

In the 1990s, the equity market in India witnessed a series of reforms, which helped in bringing it on par with international standards. However, the corporate debt market has not been able to develop due to lack of market infrastructure and a comprehensive regulatory framework. For a variety of reasons, the issuers resorted to private placement of bonds as opposed to public issues of bonds.

The corporate debt market is not yet large enough to have a significant impact on systemic stability. The Indian financial system is dominated by bank intermediation. Corporates in India have traditionally relied on borrowings from banks and financial institutions. Equity financing has also been used during periods of surging equity prices. The corporate bond market, which was reasonably vibrant in the mid-1980s, has however shrunk with respect to its alternate sources of funding. The lack of buying interest, low transparency and absence of pricing of spreads against the benchmark are some of the other reasons. The opening up of the capital account could, however, see the growth of the corporate bond market as there may be demand from foreign investors seeking exposure to high-quality corporate debt.

7.3 Emergence of Private Placement Market

In private placement, resources are raised privately through arrangers (merchant banking intermediaries) who place securities with a limited number of investors such as financial institutions, corporates and high net worth individuals. Under Section 81 of the Companies Act, 1956, a private placement is defined as 'an issue of shares or of convertible securities by a company to a select group of persons'. An offer of securities to more than 50 persons is deemed to be a public issue under the Act. Corporates access the private placement market because of its following advantages:

1. It is a cost and time-effective method of raising funds.
2. It can be structured to meet the needs of the entrepreneurs.

Private placement does not require detailed compliance of formalities as required in public or rights issues.

The emergence of private placement market has provided an easier alternative to the corporates to raise funds. Although the private placement market provides a cost-effective and time-saving mechanism for raising resources, the unbridled growth of this market has raised some concerns. The quality of issues and extent of transparency in the private placement deals remain areas of concern even though privately placed issues by listed companies are now required to be listed and also subject to necessary disclosures.

In the case of public issues, all the issues coming to the market are screened for their quality and the investors rely on ratings and other public information for evaluation of risk. Such a screening mechanism is missing in the case of private placements. This increases the risk associated with privately placed securities. Further, the private placement market appears to be growing at the expense of the public issues market, which has some distinct advantages in the form of wider participation by the investors and, thus, diversification of the risk.

The private placement market was not regulated until May 2004. In view of the mushrooming growth of the market and the risk posed by it, SEBI prescribed that the listing of all debt securities, irrespective of the mode of issuance, i.e. whether issued on a private placement basis or through public/rights issue, shall be done through a separate listing agreement. The RBI also issued guidelines to the financial intermediaries under its purview on investments in non-SLR securities, including private placement. In June 2001, boards of banks were advised to lay down policy and prudential limits on investments in bonds and debentures, including cap on unrated issues and on a private placement basis. The policy laid down by banks should prescribe stringent appraisal of issues, especially by non-borrower customers, provide for an internal system of rating, stipulate entry-level minimum ratings/quality standards and put in place proper risk management systems.

7.4 Credit Default Swaps (CDS) for Corporate Bonds

The objective of introducing CDS for corporate bonds is to

provide market participants a tool to transfer and manage credit risk in an effective manner through redistribution of risk. CDS, as a risk management product, offers the participants the opportunity to hive off credit risk and also to assume credit risk which otherwise may not be possible. Since CDS have benefits like enhancing investment and borrowing opportunities and reducing transaction costs while allowing risk transfers, such a product would increase investors' interest in corporate bonds and would be beneficial to the development of the corporate bond market in India.

Guidelines on CDS for corporate bonds were issued by the RBI on May 23, 2011, outlining broad norms including the eligible participants and other requirements. It was also indicated that market participants would have to follow the capital adequacy guidelines for CDS issued by their respective regulators. Subsequently, guidelines were issued stating that NBFCs shall participate in CDS market only as users. As users, they are permitted to buy credit protection only to hedge their credit risk on the corporate bonds they hold. They are not permitted to sell protection and hence not permitted to enter into short positions in the CDS contracts. However, they are permitted to exit their bought CDS positions by unwinding them with the original counterparty or by assigning them in favour of the buyer of the underlying bond.

7.5 Reasons for Slow Growth of Corporate Debt Market

Development of the domestic corporate debt market in India is constrained by a number of factors as listed below:

1. Low issuance leading to illiquidity in the secondary market.
2. Narrow investor base.
3. Inadequate credit assessment skills.
4. High costs of issuance.
5. Lack of transparency in trades.
6. Non-standardised instruments.
7. Comprehensive regulatory framework.

8. Underdevelopment of securitisation products.

The market suffers from deficiencies in products, participants and institutional framework. This is despite the fact that India is fairly well-placed insofar as pre-requisites for the development of the corporate bond market are concerned.

There is a reasonably well-developed government securities market, which generally precedes the development of the market for corporate debt securities. The major stock exchanges have trading platforms for the transactions in debt securities. The infrastructure also exists for clearing and settlement. The Clearing Corporation of India Limited (CCIL) has been successfully settling trades in government bonds, foreign exchange and other money market instruments. The experience with the depository system has been satisfactory. The presence of multiple rating agencies meets the requirement of an assessment framework for bond quality.

Stock markets in India have become modern and are comparable to the best in the world in terms of market infrastructure, trading and settlement practices and risk management systems. However, given the size of the Indian economy, the capital raised from the securities market has remained quite small. Corporates, by and large, tend to finance their investment activities through alternative sources, which have inhibited the growth of the market. Large and well-known corporates in India have tended to prefer international capital markets. Huge resources have also been raised by way of debt issues from the private placement market, which is less cumbersome, fast and economical. However, this segment lacks transparency and appears to be growing at the expense of the public issues segment. Lack of sufficient capital market activity has hindered the process of diversification of investment from fixed income instruments to equity-based instruments by the households.

In short, the development of the corporate bond market currently suffers from a lack of buying interest, absence of pricing of spreads against the benchmark and a flat yield curve. It requires regulatory and legislative reforms for its development.

To sum up, the development of any market requires removal of bottlenecks on supply as well as demand side, while putting in place alongside sound institutional and legal framework. In India, high economic growth has created ample demand for funds from the corporate sector which is reflected in sharp growth in bank credit and increased resource mobilisation from the international equity market and the private placement market. Encouraging business outlook and congenial investment climate have created stimulus for companies to undertake capacity expansion. On the supply side too, rising income levels and savings would require alternative investment options, including equity and corporate debt. The need, therefore, is to ensure that the capital market is well positioned to take advantage of these favourable factors.

There is a need to ensure that the corporates are able to raise resources from the capital market in a timely and cost-effective manner. The need is also felt to develop strong domestic institutional investors, which would serve many purposes. As the market evolution is an ongoing process, the Indian equity market would have to continuously strive to keep up to the international standards. In particular, corporate governance practices need to be strengthened further to raise the confidence level of a common investor. This would also enhance flow of institutional money to equities.

Even on the supply side, the need for the corporate bond market by the corporates is inadequate. This is due to their increased access to the off-shore market and improving off-shore spreads/risk perception resulting in greater liquidity off-shore rather than on-shore. Further, a sizable market is captured by the large issuance of credit risk-free government securities and issuance of low-risk subordinated debts at attractive interest rates by banks as part of their Tier II capital. While SEBI has initiated steps to simplify issuance procedures and reduce the costs of public issuance, the relative ease in raising corporate debt through private placements has resulted in the large share of private placement issuance of corporate bonds. This has rendered the corporate bond market relatively less transparent which has, in turn, impacted the liquidity of such bonds.

The secondary market in corporate bonds is limited to highly rated securities (AA and above). The wholesale debt segments of the stock exchanges have not picked up and the OTC market in corporate bonds lacks an automated order matching system and centralised settlement. The absence of DVP is another obstacle in market development. The tax deducted at source (TDS) system for corporate bonds acts as an impediment to the development of secondary market activities, especially since government securities are not subject to TDS. The delay in contract enforcement also hampers market development.

8

Money Market

8.1 Meaning, Components and Functions of Money Market

Money market is the most important segment of the financial system as it provides the fulcrum for equilibrating short-term demand for and supply of funds, thereby facilitating the conduct of monetary policy. It is a market for short-term funds with a maturity of up to one year and includes financial instruments that are close substitutes for money. [1]

Main instruments comprising the money market are as under:

- Call money/notice money.
- Certificates of deposit (CDs).
- Treasury bills.
- Repurchase agreements (repos).
- Commercial bills.
- Commercial paper (CPs).
- Inter-corporate funds.

8.1.1 Treasury Bills (T-bills): When the Central Government wants to borrow internally, it goes to the financial market. It can borrow by issuing two types of debt instruments: treasury bills and government bonds. Treasury bills are issued when the Government needs money for short period while bonds are issued when it needs money for long period.

Bill market is a sub-market of the money market in India. There are two types of bills, viz. treasury bills and commercial bills. While treasury bills are issued by the Central Government, commercial bills are issued by financial institutions.

T-bills are short-term (up to one year) money market instruments, issued by the Reserve Bank of India (RBI) on behalf of the Central Government to meet temporary liquidity shortfalls. T-bills enable investors to park their short-term surplus funds while reducing the market risk. T-bills have a maximum maturity of a 364 days. Hence, they are categorized as money market instruments (money market deals with funds with a maturity of less than one year).

T-bills are auctioned by RBI at regular intervals and issued at a discount to face value.

Presently, the active T-bills are 91-days T-bills, 182-days T-bills (now not issued) and 364-days T-bills. The 91-days and 364-days T-bills are issued on weekly auction (Wednesday) basis.

T-bills are issued on discount to face value. The holder gets the face value on maturity. The return on T-bills is the difference between the issue price and face value. Thus, return on T-bills depends upon auctions. When the liquidity position in the economy is tight, returns are higher and vice versa. For example, a 91-days T-bill of ₹ 100 (face value) may be issued at say ₹ 98.30, i.e. at a discount of ₹ 1.70 and would be redeemed at the face value of ₹ 100.

T-bills are issued only by the Central Government. State Governments do not issue any treasury bills. Treasury bills are available for a minimum amount of ₹ 25,000 and in multiples of ₹ 25,000.

Since T-bills are issued by the Government (sovereign papers), they carry zero risk. Similarly, due to their short-term maturity, they are highly liquid assets. The secondary market for T bills is very active so they have a higher degree of tradability. There is no tax deduction at source.

Individuals, firms, trusts, institutions and banks can purchase T-bills. The commercial and co-operative banks use T-bills for fulfilling their statutory liquidity ratio (SLR) requirements. T-bills are usually held by financial institutions including banks. They have a very important role in the financial market beyond investment instruments. Banks meet their SLR requirement by investing in T-bills also. Banks give T-bills to the RBI to get money under repurchase option (repo).

While inter-bank money markets and central bank lending via repo operations or discounting, provide liquidity for banks, private non-bank money market instruments, such as commercial bills and commercial paper provide liquidity to the commercial sector. Unlike in developed economies where money markets are promoted by financial intermediaries out of efficiency considerations, in India, as in many other developing countries, the evolution of the money market and its structure has been integrated into the overall deregulation process of the financial sector.

The money market is generally expected to perform three broad functions.

1. It provides an equilibrating mechanism to even out demand for and supply of short-term funds.
2. It also presents a focal point for central bank intervention for influencing liquidity and general level of interest rates in the economy.
3. It provides reasonable access to providers and users of short-term funds to fulfil their borrowing and investment requirements at an efficient market clearing price.

8.2 Reserve Bank of India (RBI) and the Money Market

The RBI is the most important constituent of the money market. Owing to its implications for conducting monetary policy, the money market falls under the direct purview of regulation of the RBI. The primary objective of the RBI's operations in the money market has been to ensure that short-term interest rates and liquidity are maintained at levels which are consistent with the overall monetary policy objectives, viz. maintaining price stability, ensuring adequate flow of credit to the productive sectors of the economy and maintaining orderly conditions in the financial markets. Liquidity and interest rates in the system are influenced by the RBI through the use of various instruments at its disposal which, *inter alia*, include the following.

1. Variations in cash reserve ratio.

2. Standing facilities/refinance schemes.
3. Repo and reverse repo transactions.
4. Changes in the Bank Rate.
5. Open market operations.
6. Foreign exchange swaps operations.

Recognising the important role of the market in the monetary policy process, the RBI has taken active interest in continuously refining the money market instruments in order to have greater control over the liquidity in the system and for creating an efficient mechanism to impart interest rate signals.

8.3 Evolution of Money Market in India

8.3.1 Pre-Independence Period: Money market prior to Independence was characterised by paucity of instruments, lack of depth and dichotomy in the market structure. The inter-bank call money market was the core of the Indian money market. Before the establishment of the RBI in 1935, the money market consisted of two fairly distinct sectors, *viz*. the organised and unorganised sectors. While the organised sector consisted of the Imperial Bank of India—a quasi-central bank till 1935, [2] the Indian joint-stock banks and the exchange banks, the indigenous bankers such as the shroffs, money lenders, chit funds etc. formed the unorganised part. Co-operative credit institutions occupied an intermediate position between the two sectors.

The Imperial Bank, the foremost commercial bank of the country and a few of the leading Indian joint-stock banks discounted *hundis* (internal bills of exchange). This was the main credit instrument of the unorganised sector which provided the only link between the two sectors. Owing to the absence of a proper central bank, the money market was characterised by sharp imbalances between the supply and demand for funds, wide fluctuations in interest rates during the busy and slack seasons and marked regional variations in interest rates. The Imperial Bank could not, however, lend stability to the money market as it had to borrow from the

Government at high rates of interest. Nevertheless, the bank rendered assistance to the money market by using the large Government balances at its disposal, which constituted its major investible resources.

The Bank Rate was the prime lending rate at which the Imperial Bank generally advanced money against Government securities. This rate was determined by the Committee of the Central Board of the Imperial Bank and depended on the demand for money which in turn was determined almost entirely by the requirements of trade, particularly foreign trade, in staple commodities such as foodgrains, raw cotton, raw jute and jute manufactures. The rates of interest on loans, including the Bank Rate, fluctuated according to the ebb and flow of this trade. The Imperial Bank would usually not reduce the Bank Rate when its cash to liabilities ratio (an indication of liquidity) was found to be low.

Apart from the Bank Rate, the Imperial Bank also periodically announced a *hundi* rate, which was generally equal to or slightly higher than the Bank Rate. Through the rates which the Imperial Bank charged on its advances and the discount of *hundis,* and by its willingness or refusal to extend financial assistance, it could profoundly influence the provision of credit as well as money market rates.

After the formation of the RBI in 1935, the organised market comprised the RBI, the Imperial Bank, foreign banks and the Indian joint stock banks. [3] *Quasi*-Government bodies and large-sized joint stock companies also participated in the money market as lenders, the money lent by them being usually termed as *house money*. Financial intermediaries such as call loan brokers, general finance and stock brokers also functioned in the market. Although the magnitude of funds dealt within the call market was not large in relation to the deposit resources of banks, it was the most sensitive segment of the money market. The Imperial Bank did not participate in the call money market, but other banks obtained loans and advances from it. Subsequently, however, banks increasingly shifted their demand for accommodation to the RBI. Besides the call money market, there was no other significant segment in the market.

With the establishment of the RBI in April 1935, the task of determining the Bank Rate was taken over by it from the Imperial Bank. It was on July 4, 1935, i.e. the day before the scheduled banks were to lodge their statutory deposits with the RBI, that the Bank Rate of 3.5 percent was officially announced for the first time by the RBI. It was the standard rate at which the RBI was prepared to buy or re-discount bills of exchange or other eligible commercial papers.

Subsequently, the official rate of the Imperial Bank was re-designated as the Imperial Bank advance rate (as distinct from the Imperial Bank *hundi* rate), which was to be the rate for advances against Government securities and the benchmark for the calculation of interest on other advances on which a fluctuating rate of interest was charged.

8.3.2 Post-Independence Period: At the time of Independence in 1947, money market structure in India was loose though not entirely uncoordinated. The indigenous bankers enjoyed rediscount facilities from the Imperial Bank and other commercial banks which, in turn, had access to the RBI. Recourse on the part of the indigenous money market to the resources of the organised market took place usually during the busy season when the crops were being harvested and moved from the producer to the wholesaler.

Though the RBI was empowered, under the statute, to use the usual instruments of monetary policy, the choice of the instruments of monetary control that could be used was limited by the structural characteristics of the money market. An important aspect of the money market in India was the seasonality in the demand for money and credit which broadly followed the course of the agricultural season. The incidence of closing of accounts of the Government at the end of the financial year in March also added to the element of seasonality in the money market.

The introduction of Bill Market Scheme by the RBI on

January 16, 1952 was a landmark in the growth of money market in India. [4] Under the scheme, the RBI made advances to scheduled banks in the form of demand loans against their promissory notes supported by 90 days usance bills or promissory notes of their constituents. It was primarily a scheme for providing accommodation to banks. The scheme, however, did not succeed in developing a market in genuine bills.

In order to serve the economy in general and the rural sector in particular, the All-India Rural Credit Survey Committee recommended the creation of the state-partnered and state-sponsored bank by taking over the Imperial Bank of India, and integrating with it, the former state-owned or state-associate banks. An Act was, accordingly, passed in the Parliament in May 1955 and the State Bank of India was constituted on July 1, 1955.

A new scheme called the Bills Rediscounting Scheme was introduced with several new features in November 1970 under which the RBI rediscounted genuine trade bills at the Bank Rate or at a rate specified by it, at its discretion. Over the years the rediscounting facility was made restrictive and made available on a discretionary basis. The other instrument in the money market was participation certificates (introduced in 1970). Both of these were, however, not significant.

Prior to financial sector reforms initiated in early 1990s, money market in India was characterised by poor liquidity, the paucity of instruments and limited number of participants. The major features of the Indian money market were the following.

1. Restricted market with a narrow base and limited number of participants—banks and two all India financial institutions. The entry into the market was tightly regulated. Moreover, the market was lopsided with a few large lenders and a large number of borrowers. The market lacked participants who could make for an active market by alternating between lending and borrowing.
2. The overall size of the market was also very small relative to the size of the economy—overall transactions barely

formed 3 to 4 percent of the bank deposits.

3. The market was also characterised by paucity of instruments and dealings were generally confined to overnight call and short notice (up to 14 days), inter-bank deposits/loans, Repo market and bills rediscounting.
4. The interest rates in the market were also tightly regulated and controlled (by a voluntary agreement between the participants through the Indian Banks' Association (IBA) intermediation). However, during periods of tight liquidity, the prescribed rates were not strictly adhered to, and more often breached.

Owing to the above features, the unorganised money market used to meet the sectoral financing gaps (i.e. the requirements of unsatisfied borrowers in the organised financial system). Interest rates in the unorganised sector were higher than those in the organised sector and were more market-related.

The Committee to Review the Working of the Monetary System in India (Chairman: Sukhamoy Chakravarty), 1985 first underlined the need to develop money market instruments in India, while the Working Group on the Money Market (Chairman: N. Vaghul), 1987 laid the blueprint for the institution of money markets. Based on the recommendations of the Chakravarty Committee and the Vaghul Working Group, the RBI has gradually developed money market in India through the following measures.

First, interest rate ceilings on inter-bank call/notice money (10 percent), inter-bank term money (10.5-11.5 percent), rediscounting of commercial bills (12.5 percent) and inter-bank participation without risk (12.5 percent) were withdrawn effective May 1, 1989.

Secondly, several financial innovations in terms of money market instruments, such as auctions of Treasury Bills (beginning with the introduction of 182-day Treasury Bills effective November 1986), certificates of deposit (June, 1989), commercial paper (January 1990) and RBI repo (December

1992) were introduced.

Thirdly, barriers to entry were gradually eased by: (a) increasing the number of players (beginning with the Discount and Finance House of India (DFHI) in April 1988 followed by primary and satellite dealers and money market mutual funds), (b) relaxing both issuance restrictions and subscription norms in respect of money market instruments and allowing determination of yields based on demand and supply of such paper, and (c) enabling market evaluation of associated risks, by withdrawing regulatory restrictions such as bank guarantees in respect of CPs.

Fourthly, the development of markets for short-term funds at market determined interest rates has been fostered by a gradual switch from a cash credit system to a loan-based system, shifting the onus of cash management from banks to borrowers and phasing out the 4.6 percent 91-day tap Treasury bills, which in the past provided an avenue for investing short-term funds.

Finally, institutional development has been carried out to facilitate inter-linkages between the money market and the foreign exchange market, especially after a market-based exchange rate system was put in place in March 1993.

8.4 Developments in the Money Market since 1991

The money market in India witnessed significant progress particularly from the mid-1990s, in terms of refinements in money market instruments, introduction of new instruments and supplementary measures to add depth and liquidity to the market.

During the 1990s, the participation in the call money market was widened to cover primary and satellite dealers and corporates (through primary dealers) besides other participants. While banks and primary dealers are permitted to lend and borrow in the market, other entities can participate only as lenders.

Following the recommendations of the Committee on Banking Sector Reforms (Chairman: M. Narasimham), 1998 and the RBI's Internal Working Group to Examine the

Development of Call Money Market (1997), steps were initiated to reform the call money market and make it a pure inter-bank market, in a phased manner starting in 1999. With the development of the repo market since the late 1990s, the call money market has gradually been transformed into a pure inter-bank market including primary dealers. This process, which was initiated in 1999, was completed in August 2005.

A significant development in the Indian money market has been the introduction of Rupee derivatives, i.e. interest rate swaps (IRS)/forward rate agreements (FRA) in 1999 to further deepen the money market and enable market participants to hedge their risks. In addition to several other measures taken since its introduction, with effect from May 20, 2005, market participants were advised to use only domestic Rupee benchmarks for interest rate derivatives. Market participants were, however, given a transition period of six months for using Mumbai inter-bank forward offered rate (MIFOR) as a benchmark, subject to review. However, on request from the Fixed Income Money Market and Derivatives Association (FIMMDA), market participants have been allowed to use MIFOR swaps in respect of transactions having underlying permissible forex exposures, for market making purpose, subject to appropriate limit as may be approved by the RBI.

Following the recommendations of the Technical Group on Money Market (May 2005), the focus and policy thrust of the RBI in the money market has been towards encouraging the growth of collateralised market, ensuring transparency and better price discovery, providing avenues for better risk management and strengthening monetary operations.

Trading in money market instruments can take place on a trading platform or in the OTC market. Electronic platforms are available for deals in the call, notice and term money market transactions, market repo and collateralised borrowing and lending obligation (CBLO). OTC deals are done for commercial paper (CP) and certificate of deposit (CD), as well as for call/notice/term money markets. Settlement is done over the real time gross settlement system—either as a gross settlement or as a multilateral netted batch. CP and CD deals, which are mostly in the form of private placements, are done OTC.

The RBI's regulatory powers over money market securities was strengthened under Clause 45(W) of the RBI Amendment Act, 2006, wherein the RBI was given specific powers to 'regulate the financial system of the country to its advantage, determine the policy relating to interest rates or interest rate products, and give directions on that behalf to all agencies or any of them, dealing in securities, money market instruments, foreign exchange, derivatives, or other instruments of like nature as the Bank may specify from time to time'.

To sum up, the money market is an important channel for monetary policy transmission and has generally conformed to being a liquid market. The gradual shift towards a collateralised inter-bank market, policy directions towards reductions in statutory reserve requirements, the introduction of new instruments such as CBLO, implementation of RTGS, significant transformation of monetary operations framework towards market-based arrangements and facilitating trading through NDS-CALL are some of the factors that have contributed to the development of a relatively vibrant and liquid money market. However, the inability of market participants to take a medium-to long-term perspective on interest rates and liquidity, coupled with the absence of a credible long-term benchmark, is a major hurdle for further market development and needs to be addressed.

Money market in India, which traditionally consisted largely of call/notice money market, now comprises many other instruments such as CPs, CDs, repos and FRAs/IRS. Various reform measures have helped in improving the depth and efficiency of money market operations. The operationalisation of the LAF has provided an informal corridor for overnight call money borrowing rate, which has further imparted stability and flexibility in the interest rate structure and to the market. The other money market instruments such as CPs and CDs have also been developed through alignment in maturity (with deposit instruments like term deposits) and easing of issuance norms. With proper development of other money market segments, non-banks have been able to smoothly switch over from the call/notice money market to other segments.

Historically, call money market has constituted the core of money market in India. However, the collateralized segments, viz., market repo and CBLO, have come into prominence recently. Market structure is broad-based with the participation of banks, primary dealers, insurance companies, mutual funds, provident funds, and corporates. Such a broad participation has contributed to an active interest across market segments.

Endnotes

1. There is no demarcated distinction between the short-term money market and the long-term capital market, and in fact there are integral links between the two markets as the array of instruments in the two markets invariably forms a continuum.
2. The Imperial Bank acted as the bankers' bank, though not statutorily, till 1935 and held the balances of other banks (both Indian and exchange) and also granted accommodation to them when in difficulty or during periods of tight money conditions. (This position remained unchanged even after 1935 in regions where the RBI had not set up offices). Advances were generally granted by way of demand loans against the Government or other gilt edged securities, though at times these were also in the nature of overdrafts.
3. As early as in 1931, the Indian Central Banking Enquiry Committee (1931) had underscored the need for integration of the two sectors of the Indian money market. It had recommended linking of indigenous bankers satisfying certain conditions such as minimum capital and reserves, nature of business, having audited accounts *etc.*, with the RBI. Subsequently, the RBI drew up a scheme in August 1937 for inclusion of indigenous bankers doing banking business under the Second Schedule of the Reserve Bank of India Act, 1934.

   At around the time the RBI was established, the unorganised money market was the most important segment accounting for as much as 90 percent of the transactions. Since then, its importance in overall terms fell considerably. But for certain sectors such as agriculture, retail trade, various classes of small borrowers and also to an extent small scale industry, this market continued to remain an important source of finance, its chief advantages being flexibility in operations and ease of access to the borrowers. But these advantages were more than offset by the highly onerous terms on which resources were made available to the borrowers. One of the most important objectives of policy at that time was, therefore, to devise methods to facilitate the flow of credit to these sectors from the organised sector and to provide it on reasonable terms.

4. Rediscounting bills were among the most important instruments of credit control and the Indian Central Banking Enquiry Committee (1931) had recommended early establishment of a market in commercial bills. No steps could, however, be taken by the RBI in this direction until the beginning of 1952 because of the War and the difficulties arising out of the partition of the country.

9

Mutual Funds

Mutual fund is a financial intermediary established in the form of a trust to utilize savings from public at large (mostly household savings) and invest the pooled fund in various instruments of capital and money market. Mutual funds are very popular all over the world and they play an important role in the financial system of many countries. Mutual funds are an ideal medium for investment by small investors in the stock market. Mutual funds pool together the investments of small investors for participation in the stock market. Being institutional investors, mutual funds can afford market analysis generally not available to individual investors. Furthermore, mutual funds can diversify the portfolio in a better way as compared with individual investors due to the expertise and availability of funds. A diversified portfolio always has a lower risk profile than a concentrated portfolio.

9.1 Types of Mutual Funds

Mutual funds can be of various types.

- **Open-ended Funds:** They are the most liquid funds. Units can be bought from and sold to the fund itself throughout the year (except book closure period), There is no fixed maturity period. Sale and purchase is at NAV-related prices which are disclosed on daily basis
- **Closed-ended Funds:** They are open for subscription only during a specific period. They are listed on stock exchange after specified period. They have a fixed maturity period (say 3 to 15 years).
- **Growth Funds:** The objective is to generate long-term capital appreciation from a portfolio.
- **Income Funds:** The objective is to generate regular

income with safety of investment.

- **Balanced Funds:** The objective is to generate capital appreciation along with current income from a balanced portfolio of equity and debt
- **Gilt Funds:** The objective is to generate risk-free returns by investments in sovereign securities issued by Central and State Governments.

9.2 Legal and Regulatory Framework

In general, the mutual fund regulatory framework in India is much more extensive and developed than in many other countries. Indian mutual funds are unit trusts, formed under the Indian Trusts Act of 1882. Their operation is governed by mutual fund regulations, totalling 78, promulgated by SEBI in exercise of the powers conferred by Section 30, read with clause (c) of sub-section (2) of Section 11 of the Securities and Exchange Board of India, Act 1992. The first set of mutual fund regulations was originally promulgated in 1996, and has since been amended from time to time. In order to remove any difficulties in the application or interpretation of these regulations, Regulation 77 of the mutual funds regulations additionally authorises SEBI to issue "clarifications and guidelines in the form of notes or circulars which shall be binding upon the sponsor, mutual funds, trustees, asset management companies and custodians".

9.3 History of Mutual Funds

Mutual funds in India were first created in 1963 when the Unit Trust of India (UTI), a state-sponsored entity, came into being. Until 1987, UTI was the only mutual fund in the country. Between 1987 and 1993 other entities belonging to the public sector were permitted to offer mutual funds—basically state-controlled banks and insurers. As part of financial sector reforms, the mutual fund industry was opened to the private sector in 1993. Thus, from 1993 onwards, private sector organisations were permitted to enter the market and the first mutual fund regulations were promulgated, which were subsequently replaced by the

SEBI (Mutual Fund) Regulations of 1996. These private sector organisations comprised both Indian and foreign joint ventures as well as purely Indian firms.

Since then, the expansion of mutual fund business has intensified competition and led to product innovation. Mutual funds presently offer a variety of options to investors such as income funds, balanced funds, liquid funds, gift funds, index funds, exchange traded funds, sectoral funds etc. The deceleration in the growth of mutual funds in the 1990s could be attributed partly to the relatively poor performance of the stock markets and partly due to withdrawal of tax benefits under Section 80M of the Indian Income Tax Act, 1961.

Some of the mutual funds had offered assured return schemes enabling them to mobilise large resources. A number of mutual funds faced difficulties in meeting their redemption obligations relating to such schemes. In several cases, the sponsors of mutual funds had to infuse additional funds to meet the shortfall. As a result, mutual funds, by and large, discontinued the floatation of assured return schemes, which had some dampening effect on the resource mobilisation by mutual funds.

9.3.1 Bifurcation of UTI: While most of the mutual funds were somehow able to meet their commitments on account of assured return schemes, UTI faced a somewhat different problem on two different occasions between October 1998 and July 2001. US-64, which was the flagship scheme of UTI and enjoyed the investors' faith, first faced problem in December 1998 when the reserves under the scheme were reported negative. In order to restore investors' confidence, several measures were initiated by the Government/UTI. While these measures helped the US-64 to make a turnaround, the problem resurfaced again in July 2001 when UTI slashed down the dividend rates for the year 2000-01 and suspended sales and repurchases of US-64 for a period of 6 months from July 2001 to December 2001. This created a crisis of confidence and to restore investors' confidence various measures were initiated again, which culminated in splitting the UTI into two parts.

On October 28, 2002, an ordinance was promulgated which repealed the UTI Act, and bifurcated UTI into two separate entities. One is the Specified Undertaking of the Unit Trust of India. The Specified Undertaking of Unit Trust of India, functioning under an administrator and under the rules framed by Government of India and does not come under the purview of the mutual fund regulations. It has US-64 and the assured returns schemes. The second is the UTI Mutual Fund Ltd., sponsored by State Bank of India (SBI), Bank of Baroda (BoB), Punjab National Bank (PNB) and Life Insurance Corporation of India (LIC). It is registered with SEBI and functions under the mutual fund regulations. It is an unencumbered mutual fund, with only NAV-based schemes.

The problem with US-64 scheme of UTI adversely affected the resource mobilisation by mutual funds in general and UTI in particular. On both the occasions, when UTI faced difficulties and while resource mobilisation by UTI declined sharply, private sector mutual funds were able to fill the gap created by UTI only partially as overall mobilisation by all mutual funds on both the occasions declined sharply after the occurrence of the problem.

In March 2002, guidelines were issued to enable mutual funds to invest in rated securities in countries with fully convertible currencies. This marked an important milestone, through which mutual funds will be able to deliver better risk/return tradeoffs through international diversification.

9.4 Features of Mutual Fund Industry in India

These are as under:

1. Mutual funds are popular mainly with the middle and high-income groups.
2. Investors are largely based in the urban centres, particularly the metropolitan cities.
3. Penetration of mutual funds in the rural areas remains small.

4. UTI and other state-owned asset management companies have lost market share, while private sector funds have grown rapidly.
5. Asset management companies are divided into those that are predominantly owned by the state (UTI, bank sponsored and institutions) and those that are in the private sector.
6. Mutual fund industry has to compete with attractive assured returns from Government schemes and this is possibly the single most important impediment to the growth of the industry.

Thus, if mutual funds have to grow fast, they would need to devise appropriate schemes to attract the saving of low-income groups, especially in rural areas. This is the only way to ensure participation of all categories of investors into the capital market, which is so crucial for its long-term development.

9.5 Problems of Mutual Funds

India has a high household savings ratio. Indians, like most people anywhere, are conservative in their habits, and it would take many years to change this behaviour, particularly when it comes to the use of their savings. As in most countries, investment in physical assets (mainly housing and gold) accounts for the most important percentage of household assets. Owning a home is usually a first priority once a family has any disposable income at all.

9.5.1 Competition with Government Schemes: Mutual funds compete against a host of high yielding government-backed savings schemes such as public provident fund (PPF), national savings scheme (NSS), RBI bonds, and so on, as well as against life insurance products and, in the future, against the new pension schemes for the unorganised sector. [1] The political and social reasons for keeping yields higher than the market for small savers, particularly retired savers, is understandable. The market is distorted by such a policy. Government should have the strategic aim of discontinuing over time or at least reducing the availability of the unrealistically high yielding avenues for small savings. The objective of widening and deepening ownership of mutual funds is unlikely to be met until this happens.

Fixed income and balanced mutual funds have offered a reasonably competitive rate of return but they are not guaranteed, a key attraction to Indian investors. The net result is that mutual funds fail to attract much money from retail investors, who prefer to invest in a no-risk, high return product, i.e. government saving schemes or provident funds or keep their money safely in the bank.

Government-sponsored instruments *crowd out* mutual funds since for the majority of Indians buying mutual funds, before they have their full complement of government-backed savings instruments, would be both wrong and foolish.

In most countries government guaranteed financial instruments offer returns that are likely to be significantly lower than private sector investments available from mutual funds or insurance companies. This is the penalty that investors are prepared to pay for little or no risk. However, Indian retail investors are not being asked to sacrifice any substantial amount of return in exchange for a government guarantee.

Conversely, returns on government assured investments are often better than those available elsewhere. While conventional government bonds do give lower returns than equivalent private sector corporate bonds, the retail government assured products give higher returns for almost no risk. It is thus hardly surprising that an investor of modest means would choose to invest in, for instance, national savings certificates, since he can thus obtain a better return for a much lower risk. Any investor would be well advised to invest the maximum permitted in the various government assured schemes before considering other forms of investment.

The reasons why the government is prepared to pay above market rates of interest on certain financial products is understandable. At a time when interest rates have fallen substantially from their previous levels, savers who had counted on the interest on their savings to provide an income, particularly in retirement, are being subsidised. Given that pension arrangements, particularly in the unorganised sector, are not widespread, such an approach is reasonable and indeed most small savers are acting rationally when they choose the low risk option. However, this approach conflicts with a desire to widen and deepen participation in capital markets through mutual funds or other non-governmental savings products by the less well-off sectors of the population.

9.5.2 Competition from Insurance: The take up life assurance is growing rapidly and may be pre-empting some of the market that mutual funds could aim at. Life assurance is an easier product to sell, since in the mind of the investor the payment of a premium is often linked to a specific outcome, a lump sum payment on death or a guaranteed minimum sum on maturity. It also pays higher commissions to sales agents (typically the amount of the first 5 to 6 months premium). Thus, a sales agent will usually prefer to sell a life policy since it will reward him better.

9.5.3 Volatility of Mutual Fund Performance: There is a perception that mutual funds have somehow let down their investors and given them poor returns. In July 2001 when UTI slashed down the dividend rates for the year 2000-01 and suspended sales and repurchases of US-64 for a period of 6 months from July 2001 to December 2001, it created a crisis of confidence among the investors with long-term effects.

9.5.4 Tax System Encourages Short-term Objectives: Mutual funds are regarded in most countries as a diversified, professionally managed and well-regulated vehicle for mobilising household savings and are often accorded tax privileges specifically in pursuit of a government policy goal to encourage long-term savings, notably for retirement. [2] It is unusual for such tax privileges to impel mutual funds towards short-term goals, which is what seems to be the case in India. True, Indian unit trusts are diversified, professionally managed and well-regulated, but they are certainly not serving long-term objectives.

9.6 Mutual Funds and the Stock Market

Mutual funds in India, because of their small size and slower growth in the recent past, have tended to play only a limited role in the stock market. In view of small size of their operations, mutual funds in normal times hardly exert any influence on the stock market. Mutual funds with large funds at their disposal are expected by the government to act as a counterweight to foreign institutional investors (FIIs), which generally exert a significant influence on the stock market. Some leading asset management companies in India are listed in Table 9.1.

Table 9.1: Leading Asset Management Companies in India (as in June 2019)

S. No.	Name of the Company
Bank Sponsored	
1.	BOI AXA Investment Managers Pvt. Ltd.
2.	Canara Robeco Asset Management Co. Ltd.
3.	SBI Funds Management Pvt. Ltd.
4.	Union Asset Management Co. Pvt. Ltd.
5.	Baroda Asset Management India Ltd.
6.	IDBI Asset Management Ltd.
7.	UTI Asset Management Co. Ltd.
Institutions (Indian)	
1.	IIFCL Asset Management Co. Ltd.
2.	LIC Mutual Fund Asset Management Ltd.
Private Sector (Indian)	
1.	DSP Investment Managers Pvt. Ld.
2.	Edelweiss Asset Management Ltd.
3.	Essel Finance AMC Ltd.
4.	IDFC Asset Management Co. Ltd.
5.	IIFL Asset Management Ltd.
6.	IL&FS Infra Asset Management Ltd.

Contd…

7.	Indiabulls Asset Management Co. Ltd.
8.	ITI Asset Management Ltd.
9.	JM Financial Asset Management Ltd.
10.	Kotak Mahindra Asset Management Co. Ltd.
11.	L&T Investment Management Ltd.
12.	Mahindra Asset Management Co. Pvt. Ltd.
13.	Motilal Oswal Asset Management Co. Ltd.
14.	PPFAS Asset Management Pvt. Ltd.
15.	Quant Money Managers Ltd.
16.	Quantum Asset Management Co. Pvt. Ltd.
17.	Sahara Asset Management Co. Pvt. Ltd.
18.	Shriram Asset Management Co. Ltd.
19.	SREI Mutual Fund Asset Management Pvt. Ltd.
20.	Sundaram Asset Management Co. Ltd.
21.	Tata Asset Management Ltd.
22.	Taurus Asset Management Co. Ltd.
23.	YES Asset Management (India) Ltd.
Private Sector (Foreign)	
1.	BNP Paribas Asset Management India Pvt. Ltd.
2.	Franklin Templeton Asset Management India Pvt. Ltd.
3.	HSBC Asset Management (India) Pvt. Ltd.
4.	Invesco Asset Management (India) Pvt. Ltd.
5.	Mirae Asset Global Investments (India) Pvt. Ltd.
6.	Principal Asset Management Pvt. Ltd.
Joint Ventures (Predominantly Indian)	
1.	Aditya Birla Sun Life AMC Ltd.
2.	Axis Asset Management Co. Ltd.
3.	HDFC Asset Management Co. Ltd.
4.	ICICI Prudential Asset Management Co. Ltd.
5.	Reliance Nippon Life Asset Management Ltd.
Joint Ventures (Others)	
1.	DHFL Pramerica Asset Managers Pvt. Ld.

Source: www.amfiindia.com.

Table 9.2 presents the value of assets under management

of mutual funds in India.

Table 9.2: Assets under Management of Mutual Funds: 2000-2019

S. No.	**Year** (ending March 31)	**Amount** (₹ crore)
1.	2000	1,07,946
2.	2001	90,587
3.	2002	1,00,954
4.	2003	1,09,229
5.	2004	1,39,616
6.	2005	1,49,600
7.	2006	2,31,862
8.	2007	3,26,292
9.	2008	5,05,152
10.	2009	4,17,300
11.	2010	6,13,979
12.	2011	5,92,250
13.	2012	5,87,217
14.	2013	7,01,443
15.	2014	8,25,240
16.	2015	10,82,757
17.	2016	12,32,824
18.	2017	17,54,619
19.	2018	21,36,036
20.	2019	23,79,584
21.	**As on May 31, 2019**	**25,93,559**

Sources: www.rbi.org and www.amfiindia.com.

To sum up, the mutual fund industry in India is quite sophisticated and successful. It is dominated by good and reputable institutions, both Indian and international. Nevertheless improvements are always possible and desirable in order to enhance the ability of the mutual fund industry to mobilise savings on a wider scale and to contribute to the further development of capital market.

Endnotes

1. Many of the government assured schemes are probably not fulfilling their original purpose. For example the Public Provident Fund (PPP) was set up in 1968-69 with the objective of providing unorganised sector workers with a facility to accumulate savings for old age income security. As a result of premature withdrawal facilities and tax breaks, individuals largely misuse this scheme for legitimised tax evasion and it does not serve the intended purpose of old age income security.
2. There is no perfect system for taxing the income and gains of mutual funds and their investors. The main principle that almost all regimes follow is that there should be broadly equality of treatment between all mutual fund investors and between mutual fund investors and direct investors in securities. In other words, an investor purchasing assets indirectly through a mutual fund should be no worse off tax-wise than if that same investor bought those assets directly on their own behalf. This is the principle of *fiscal neutrality*.

   The taxation of funds is a key issue for funds and their management companies. Taxation affects both the attractiveness of funds compared with other investments, and also the systems that may have to be designed and implemented in order for funds to operate efficiently and cost effectively. Fund managers in virtually every market in the world lobby governments hard either to remove tax disadvantages or to achieve favourable treatment, so that their product can become more competitive in the market and more attractive to potential buyers.

10

Portfolio Investment by Foreign Institutional Investors (FIIs)

In India, foreign portfolio investor (FPI) means a person registered in accordance with the provisions of Securities and Exchange Board of India (SEBI) (Foreign Portfolio Investors) Regulations, 2014, as amended from time to time. Similarly, foreign institutional investor (FII) means an entity established or incorporated outside India which proposes to make investment in India and which is registered as a FII in accordance with the Securities and Exchange Board of India (SEBI) (Foreign Institutional Investor) Regulations, 1995.

Portfolio investment occurs when individual investors invest, mostly through stockbrokers, in stocks of foreign companies in foreign land in search of profit opportunities.

Institutional investors are specialised financial intermediaries managing savings collectively on behalf of investors, especially small investors, towards specific objectives in terms of risk, returns, and maturity of claims.

One of the major forces changing the face and structure of international capital markets since 1990s has been the flow of cross-border portfolio investments—especially by foreign institutional investors (FIIs), from developed countries to the developing countries. Portfolio investors provide institutional character to the capital markets, flavoured by highly intensive research and diversified investments. FII investments inject global liquidity into the markets, raise the price-earning ratio and thus reduce the cost of capital. From the perspective of FIIs, investments in various countries provide a measure of portfolio diversification and hedging as also to take advantage of arbitrage opportunities.

FIIs make investments in various countries to provide a

measure of portfolio diversification and hedging to their assets. The forces driving the recent change in the investment portfolio of FIIs, as reflected in the growing emphasis on equities of emerging market economies, include *inter alia*: (a) increased accessibility of these markets after liberalisation, (b) improved marketability, (c) fewer problems relating to thin trading and (d) improved macroeconomic fundamentals of these countries.

10.1 Advantages of Portfolio Investment Inflows

Following are the chief advantages of having investments by foreign institutional investors (FIIs).

10.1.1 Improvement in Corporate Capital Structure: FIIs are well-known for a greater appetite for equity than debt in their asset structure. Thus, opening up the economy to FIIs is in line with the accepted preference for non-debt creating foreign inflows over foreign debt. Furthermore, because of this preference for equities over bonds, FIIs can help in compressing the yield-differential between equity and bonds and improve corporate capital structure.

10.1.2 Competition in Financial Markets: Institutional investors promote financial innovation and development of hedging instruments. Institutions, for example, because of their interest in hedging risks, are known to have contributed to the development of zero-coupon bonds and index futures. FIIs, as professional bodies of asset managers and financial analysts, not only enhance competition in financial markets, but also improve the alignment of asset prices to fundamentals.

Institutions in general and FIIs in particular are known to have good information and low transaction costs. By aligning asset prices closer to fundamentals, they stabilize markets. Fundamentals are known to be sluggish in their movements. Thus, if prices are aligned to fundamentals, they should be as stable as the fundamentals themselves. Furthermore, FIIs with a variety of risk-return preferences also help in dampening volatility.

10.1.3 Enhanced Efficiency in Capital Markets: FIIs as professional bodies of asset managers and financial analysts enhance competition and efficiency of financial markets. Equity market development aids economic development. By increasing the availability of riskier long-term capital for projects, FIIs can help in the process of economic development.

10.1.4 Improvement in Corporate Governance: Good corporate governance is essential to overcome the principal-agent problem between shareholders and management. Information asymmetries and incomplete contracts between share-holders and management are at the root of the agency costs. Bad corporate governance makes equity finance a costly option.

FIIs contribute to better understanding of operations and improve corporate governance of firms. Institutions are known for challenging excessive executive compensation, and removing under performing managers. There is some evidence that institutionalization increases dividend payouts, and enhances productivity growth.

10.2 Disadvantages of Portfolio Investment Inflows

Among others, the two common apprehensions about FIIs inflows are the fear of management takeovers and potential capital outflows.

10.2.1 Management Control: FIIs act as agents on behalf of their principals as financial investors maximising returns. There are domestic laws that effectively prohibit institutional investors from taking management control. In India, all takeovers are governed by SEBI's Substantial Acquisition of Shares and Takeovers Regulations, 1997, and sub-accounts of FIIs are deemed to be *persons acting in concert* with other persons in the same category unless the contrary is established. In addition, reporting requirements have been imposed on FIIs and currently *participatory notes* cannot be issued to unregulated entities abroad.

10.2.2 Volatility of Portfolio Flows: FIIs inflows are popularly described as *hot money* because of the herd behaviour and potential for large capital outflows. Herd behaviour means FIIs trying to either only buy or only sell at the same time, particularly at times of market stress. Value at risk models followed by FIIs may destabilise markets by leading to simultaneous sale by various FIIs. Extrapolative expectations or trend chasing, rather than focusing on fundamentals, can lead to destabilization.

It has been argued that under the process of globalisation, highly diversified investors participate in cross-border movement of capital. Such investors pay little attention to economic fundamentals and in the presence of asymmetric information they resort to herd behaviour, which results in volatility of international capital flows. Such a view has, however, been challenged and it has been argued that there is high level of substitutability between various forms of foreign capital.

Countries with modest growth potentials and semi-developed financial market infrastructure are most vulnerable to reversal of portfolio investment flows. Existence of large asymmetry of information in such countries can lead to sharp changes in portfolio and private debt flows in the face of even a slight change in investor perception about the health of the recipient economy. This type of volatility is, however, not limited to portfolio flows. Even external commercial borrowings, in the form of bank borrowing or bond financing, show similar patterns.

10.2.3 Pro-cyclical: The most important disadvantage of FII flows is that it tends to be pro-cyclical, in the sense that it comes in when the balance of payments (BOP) position is seen to be strong and goes out when the BOP position is expected to weaken. Thus, it accentuates the direction of movement of the BOP, which can cause serious problems in macroeconomic management. In the case of countries like India, where the foreign exchange markets are very thin as compared to the international financial market, a free FII regime carries the danger of speculative movements, which can lead to serious disruption in the economy.

10.2.4 Hedge Funds: Hedge funds are another source of concern which (unlike pension funds, life insurance companies and mutual funds) engage in short-term trading, take short positions and borrow more aggressively.

Mexican crisis and more recently the East Asian crisis have highlighted the downside risks of such flows. The downside risks include political risk, currency risk, problems associated with low liquidity and volatility on returns. Cross-country studies indicate that reversal of portfolio flows could be disorderly and result in substantial economic hardship for developing countries.

10.3 Liberalisation of Portfolio Investment Flows into India

Prior to 1992, only non-resident Indians (NRIs) and overseas corporate bodies (OCBs) were allowed to undertake portfolio investment in India. In line with the recommendations of the High Level Committee on Balance of Payments (Chairman: C. Rangarajan), FIIs were allowed to invest in the Indian debt and equity market. FII investments first started flowing into India in 1993. Portfolio investment inflows have since then been substantial.

10.3.1 Investments by FIIs: India embarked on a gradual shift towards capital account convertibility with the launch of the reforms in the early 1990s. Although foreign natural persons—except NRIs—are prohibited from investing in financial assets, such investments are permitted by FIIs and overseas corporate bodies (OCBs) with suitable restrictions. From September 14, 1992, FIIs were allowed to invest in all the securities traded on the primary and secondary markets, including shares, debentures and warrants issued by companies which were listed or were to be listed on the stock exchanges in India and in the schemes floated by domestic mutual funds. Funds invested by FIIs must have at least 50 participants with no one holding more than 5 percent to ensure a broad base and preventing such investment acting as a camouflage for individual investment in the nature of FDI and requiring Government approval.

The idea of allowing FIIs was that they were broad-based, diversified funds, leaving out individual foreign investors and foreign companies. The only exceptions were the NRI and OCB portfolio investments through the secondary market, which were subject to individual ceilings of 5 percent to prevent a possible *takeover*. Individuals were left out because of the difficulties in checking on their antecedents, and of their lack of expertise in market matters and relatively short-term perspective. OCB investments through the portfolio route were banned in November 2001.

During 1992-93, Government allowed reputed FIIs including pension funds, mutual funds, asset management companies, investment trusts nominee companies and incorporated or institutional portfolio managers to invest in the Indian capital market subject to the condition that they registered with the Securities and Exchange Board of India (SEBI) and obtained RBI approval under FERA.

In 1996-97, the guidelines for investment by FIIs were further liberalised. The limit of investment for an individual FII was raised from 5 percent to 10 percent subject, however, to the aggregate limit of 24 percent for all FIIs. The FIIs were also allowed to invest in unlisted companies in the same manner as they were allowed to invest in listed companies. FII investments in debt securities of companies as 100 percent debt funds were allowed subject to certain guidelines. FIIs were also allowed to invest in the gilt-edged government securities with the framework of guidelines. FIIs were also allowed to invest in the gilt-edged government securities within the framework of guidelines, and proprietary funds have been allowed to invest in the country through the FII route.

As a follow up of the announcement made in the Union Budget 1997-98, aggregate investment ceilings for FIIs and non-resident Indians (including OCBs) were increased up to 30 percent subject to approval by the company's shareholders.

Guidelines for foreign investment in preference shares issued by the Indian companies were also issued. These provided greater flexibility to Indian corporations in using preference shares as a form of financing. FIIs were also permitted to purchase/sell Treasury Bills within the overall approved debt ceilings.

A number of liberalization measures were taken in 1998-99 to promote portfolio foreign investment. In order to avoid NRIs being crowded out by FIIs, the aggregate ceiling for investment in a company by all NRIs/PIOs/OCBs through stock exchanges was made separate and exclusive of the investment ceiling available for FIIs. In addition, the aggregate investment ceiling for NRIs/PIOs/OCBs was raised from 5 percent to 10 percent of the paid-up capital of a company. In the case of listed Indian companies, the ceiling was raised to 24 percent of the paid-up capital under a General Body Resolution. Also, the investment limit by a single NRI/PIO/OCB was enhanced from 1 percent to 5 percent of the paid up capital. Policy pertaining to investment in unlisted companies was liberalised. NRIs/PIOs/OCBs were permitted to invest in unlisted companies.

FIIs were allowed to purchase and sell Government Securities and Treasury Bills within overall approved debt ceilings. To facilitate better risk management by investors, authorised dealers were permitted to provide forward cover to FIIs in respect of their fresh equity investments in India. Moreover, transactions among FIIs with respect to Indian stocks were no longer required post-facto conformation from the RBI. Also, 100 percent FII debt funds were permitted to invest in unlisted debt securities of Indian companies.

In March 1999, the RBI issued a notification granting general permission to mutual funds for issuing units to NRIs/PIOs/OCBs subject to certain specified norms, thereby dispensing with the existing procedure of obtaining prior permission. In addition, approval procedures were simplified by the RBI in respect of NRIs/PIOs/OCBs by granting them general permission in lieu of case by case approval procedure in a large number of areas. This included acceptance of deposits by Indian companies, investment in air taxi operations, sale of shares in stock exchanges, transfer of shares in stock exchanges, transfer of share/bonds/debentures and immovable properly to charitable trusts/organisations in India as gift, raising of loans by resident individuals/proprietorship concerns on non-repatriable basis, issue of Commercial Papers by Indian companies to NRIs etc.

In 1999-2000, with a view to expand the FIIs category, the Government permitted foreign corporates and high net worth individuals to invest through SEBI registered FIIs. Such investments were subject to a sub-limit of 5 percent within the aggregate limit for FII portfolio investments of 24 percent in a single company. Government also permitted SEBI registered domestic fund managers to manage foreign funds for investment in the Indian capital market through the portfolio investment route provided the funds were channelled through internationally recognised financial institutions and subject to the reporting requirements as applicable to FIIs.

In 2000-01, FIIs were permitted greater leverage in the primary/secondary markets by allowing enhancement of the aggregate FII investment ceiling in the issued and paid-up capital of Indian companies from the normal ceiling of 24 percent to 40 percent subject to prescribed procedures. The list of activities of non-banking financial companies (NBFCs) eligible for foreign equity investment was increased to 18 with the addition of micro-credit/rural credit. Foreign investment guidelines for NBFCs were amended for providing a minimum capitalisation norm of US$ 0.5 million for activities, which were not fund-based or consultative in nature, irrespective of the foreign equity participation level. The provision applied to investment advisory services, credit reference and rating agencies, financial consultancy, foreign exchange broking and money changing. Permission was granted to holding companies in NBFC activities with minimum capital of US$ 5 million, subject to specific conditions of disinvestment.

In order to provide stimulus to the growth of the venture capital industry in India, SEBI was made the single point nodal agency for registration of both domestic and overseas venture capital funds. Venture capital companies/funds were allowed to invest through the automatic route, subject to SEBI regulations and sector specific caps on FDI.

In February 2000, the FII regulations were amended to permit foreign corporates and high net worth individuals to also invest as sub-accounts of SEBI-registered FIIs. Foreign corporates and high net worth individuals fall outside the category of diversified investors. FIIs were also permitted to seek SEBI registration in respect of sub-accounts for their clients under the regulations. [1]

While initially FIIs were permitted to manage the sub-account of clients, the domestic portfolio managers or domestic asset management companies were also allowed to manage the funds of such sub-accounts and also to make application on behalf of such sub-accounts. Such sub-accounts could be an institution, or a fund, or a portfolio established or incorporated outside India, or a broad-based fund, or a proprietary fund, or even a foreign corporate or individual. So, in practice there are common categories of entities, which could be registered as both FIIs and sub-accounts. However, investment into a sub-account is to be made either by FIIs, or by domestic portfolio manager or asset management company, and not by itself directly.

In view of the concerns of some unregulated entities taking positions in the stock market through the mechanism of participatory notes (PNs) issued by FIIs, the issue was examined by the Ministry of Finance in consultation with RBI and SEBI. Following these consultations, in January 2004, SEBI stipulated that PNs are not to be issued to any non-regulated entity, and the principle of *know your clients* may be strictly adhered to. SEBI has indicated that the existing non-eligible PNs, would be permitted to expire or to be wound-down on maturity, or within a period of 5 years, whichever is earlier. Besides, reporting requirement on a regular basis has been imposed on all the FIIs.

In his 2011-12 budget speech, the Finance Minister further liberalized the portfolio investment route. He announced, "Currently, only FIIs and sub-accounts registered with the SEBI and NRIs are allowed to invest in mutual fund schemes. To liberalise the portfolio investment route, it has been decided to permit SEBI registered Mutual Funds to accept subscriptions from foreign investors who meet the KYC requirements for equity schemes. This would enable Indian mutual funds to have direct access to foreign investors and widen the class of foreign investors in Indian equity market". [2]

10.3.2 Equity Capital from Foreign Sources by Indian Corporates: Indian corporates are also allowed to access equity capital from foreign sources in the form of ADR/GDR and Euro issues. Policies on international offerings on ADRs/GDRs have been liberalised substantially and corporates are allowed to raise funds by way of ADRs/GDRs under automatic route, subject to specified guidelines.

Two-way fungibility in ADR/GDR issues of Indian companies has been introduced under which investors in India can purchase shares and deposit them with an Indian custodian for issue of ADRs/GDRs by the overseas depository to the extent of the ADRs/GDRs converted into underlying shares.

Indian corporate sector has been encouraged to access global capital markets through GDRs:

1. Foreign investors can invest in Indian companies through the GDR route without any lock-in period.
2. These receipts can be listed on any of the overseas stock exchanges and denominated in any convertible foreign currency. However, the underlying shares are denominated in Indian Rupees.
3. Private placement with US investors is also permissible in accordance with the US Securities Act.
4. Short-term capital gains are taxable at the rate of 65 percent along with business income.

5. Long-term capital gains (computed on holdings for more than 12 months) are taxable at the rate of 10 percent.

Guidelines for Euro-issues were liberalised in June 1996. The requirement of consistently good record of performance for 3 years was relaxed for companies wanting to raise GDRs or foreign currency convertible bonds (FCCBs) for financing investment in infrastructure. Restrictions on the number of issues that can be floated by an individual company or a group of companies during a financial year have been withdrawn.

Earlier norms regarding end-uses of GDRs have been relaxed to include financing of import of capital goods, capital expenditure including domestic purchase/installation of plant, equipment and building, investments in software development, prepayments scheme entailing repayment of earlier external borrowings, investments abroad where these have been approved by competent authorities, and equity investment in joint ventures (JVs)/wholly-owned subsidiaries (WOs) in India. A company raising GDRs can use the proceeds up to the extent of 25 percent for the purpose of meeting working capital requirements and general corporate restructuring. Furthermore, banks, financial institutions and non-banking finance companies registered with the RBI may raise GDRs without making reference to any end-uses. However, investment in the stock market and real estate is not permitted out of GDR proceeds.

GDR/ADR guidelines were further liberalised in 1998-99. Unlisted companies were permitted to float Euro issues under certain conditions. All end-use restrictions on GDR/ADR issues proceeds were removed, except the prevailing restrictions on investment in stock markets and real estate. The 90-day validity period for final approvals of GDR/ADR issues was withdrawn and final approval was continued to be valid, thereby imparting greater flexibility to issuing companies regarding the timing of issues. Indian companies were permitted to issue GDRs/ADRs in the case of bonus or right issue of shares, or on genuine business reorganisations. The companies, however, in all such cases, were required to get approval from the Department of Economic Affairs, Ministry of Finance, Government of India for the issue of GDRs/ADRs.

Considering the enhanced opportunities of Indian software companies for expanding globally, operational norms—governing their overseas investments and mode of financing acquisition of overseas software companies—were issued through a notification by the Ministry of Finance. It permitted Indian software companies, which were listed in foreign exchanges and had already floated ADR/GDR issues, to acquire foreign software companies and issue ADRs/GDRs without reference to the Government of India or the RBI up to the value limit of US$ 100 million. For acquisitions beyond US$ 100 million, proposals required examination by a Special Composite Committee in the RBI.

With a view to further liberalise the operational guidelines for ADR/GDR issues, it was decided to dispense with the track record scrutiny process for ADR/GDR issues and the two-stage approval by the Ministry of Finance. Indian companies were allowed to access the ADR/GDR markets through an automatic route without the prior approval of the Ministry of Finance subject to the specified norms and post-issue reporting requirement.

Furthermore, overseas business acquisitions through the ADR/GDR route were permitted under the automatic/simplified approval mechanism for Indian companies engaged in: (a) information technology and entertainment software; (b) pharmaceuticals; (c) biotechnology and (d) any other sector as notified by the Government from time to time.

The automatic approvals was made subject to conditions of previous listing, conformation to FDI policy and limiting of transactions to US$ 100 million or ten times the export earnings during the preceding financial year. Indian companies, engaged in IT software and IT services, were permitted to issue ADR/GDR linked stock options to permanent employees (including Indian and overseas working directors) of its subsidiary companies incorporated in India or outside and engaged in IT software and IT services. In order to encourage greater skill development in knowledge-based Indian firms, Indian companies engaged in information technology and entertainment software, pharmaceuticals, biotechnology, and any other activities within the knowledge-based sector were permitted to issue ESOPs (Employees' Stock Options) to their permanent employees. The liberalised norms for ESOPs were extended to multi-product diversified companies subject to specific conditions.

Government continued its policy of liberalising the guidelines for issue of GDRs/ADRs in a phased manner. The initiatives taken in 2001-02 included the following:

1. As a follow up of the announcement in the Budget for 2001-02, Indian companies were permitted to list in foreign stock exchanges by sponsoring ADR/GDR issues with overseas depository against shares held by its shareholders subject to prescribed conditions.
2. All companies that had made an ADR/GDR issue earlier and listed abroad were permitted the facility of overseas business acquisition through ADR/GDR stock swap under the automatic route subject to conditions that included adherence to FDI policy and the value limit for the transaction not to exceed US$ 100 million or 10 times the export earnings during the proceeding financial year.

10.4 Eligibility for Registration as FII

The following entities, established or incorporated abroad, are eligible to be registered as FIIs:

1. Pension funds.
2. Mutual funds.
3. Investment trusts.
4. Asset management companies.
5. Nominee companies.
6. Banks.
7. Institutional portfolio managers.

8. Trustees.
9. Power of attorney holders.
10. University funds, endowments, foundations or charitable trusts or charitable societies.

Besides the above, a domestic portfolio manager or domestic asset management company is also eligible to be registered as an FII to manage the funds of sub-accounts. The FIIs can also invest on behalf of sub-accounts. The following entities are entitled to be registered as sub-accounts:

1. An institution or fund or portfolio established or incorporated outside India.
2. A foreign corporate or a foreign individual.

FIIs registered with SEBI fall under the following categories:

1. **Regular FIIs:** Those who are required to invest not less than 70 percent of their investment in equity-related instruments and up to 30 percent in non-equity instruments.
2. **100 percent debt-fund FIIs:** Those who are permitted to invest only in debt instruments.

10.5 Restrictions on Foreign Portfolio Investments

Quite apart from the ceilings on FII investments, there are ceilings on FDI, and in some cases, unified ceilings for non-resident investments. There are two types of ceilings on FII investments: statutory and administrative.

There are also sectors where administrative caps for non-resident investments have been prescribed. In these sectors (viz. telecom services, media, private sector banks) FDI plus portfolio investments by FIIs and NRIs cannot exceed the administrative caps fixed.

Caps can be of 3 types:

1. A separate cap on FDI.
2. A separate cap on FII.
3. A composite cap on FDI and FII combined together.

Separate caps on FDI and FII, in turn, can be of 5 types:

1. Ban on both FDI and FII (e.g. lottery business, gambling

and betting).
2. Non-zero separate caps on both FDI and FII (e.g. DTH-broadcasting).
3. A composite non-zero cap on FDI and FII (e.g. banking, insurance, telecom).
4. Ban on FDI with a non-zero cap on FII (e.g. Terrestrial broadcasting FM, retail trading).
5. Ban on FII with a non-zero cap on FDI (e.g. print media).

FIIs have a natural advantage in processing information. One of the problems noted for such investment in emerging markets consists in the lower amount of reliable and quality information available in such countries relative to developed ones. It can be expected that with rapid progress in disclosure norms, accounting standards, shareholder rights, legal framework, and corporate governance in general, FII investments are going to accelerate in India. FII investments in some companies are already at their ceiling level, and the ceiling is much below the stakes that FIIs have acquired in some other Asian countries. Against this background, further relaxations by India may considerably enhance the attractiveness of India as a destination for foreign portfolio flows.

Trends in portfolio investment flows into India are shown in Table 10.1.

To sum up, policies relating to portfolio investment in India have been substantially liberalised since the early 1990s.

Studies show that volatility of cross-border portfolio investment flows into India has been less than what has been experienced by other emerging market economies (EMEs). The stability in portfolio flows to India has been attributed to factors such as robust economic performance since early 1990s and relatively low level of co-movements between Indian and global stock prices. Empirical estimates indicate that FII flows are positively related to returns on BSE Sensex.

FII flows into India display seasonality, with inflows being significantly higher in the first four months of each calendar year. This could be due to global factors such as money flowing into the market at the start of the year from tax saving investments and from year-end bonuses. The pattern might also reflect improved domestic sentiment, since reforms are typically announced in the run-up to the end-February Union Budget.

Table 10.1: Trends in Net Portfolio Investment Flows into India: 2000-01 to 2017-18

(US$ million)

Year	Net Portfolio Investment	Year	Net Portfolio Investment
2000-01	2,590	2009-10	32,396
2001-02	1,952	2010-11	30,293
2002-03	944	2011-12	17,170
2003-04	11,356	2012-13	26,891
2004-05	9,287	2013-14	4,822
2005-06	12,494	2014-15	42,205
2006-07	7,060	2015-16	-4,130
2007-08	27,433	2016-17	7,612
2008-09	-14,030	2017-18	22,115

Negative (-) sign indicates outflow.
Source: Reserve Bank of India, *Handbook of Statistics on Indian Economy,* 2017-18, Table 150 (excerpted).

Various supply and demand factors have made investing via institutions a rapidly growing sector in many developed countries. There is enhanced supply of funds from investors to institutions because of the aging of population, funded pension systems, and growing wealth. Institutions are also able to give better services and attractive returns because of ease of diversification, better corporate governance, liquidity, deregulation and fiscal incentives. Given this background, there is likely to be a large and growing demand for Indian stocks by FIIs.

Endnotes

1. While permitting foreign corporates/high net worth individuals in February 2000 to invest through SEBI registered FII/domestic fund managers, it was noted that there was a clear distinction

between portfolio investment and FDI. The basic presumption is that FIIs are not interested in management control. To allay fears of management control being exercised by portfolio investors, it was noted that adequate safety nets were in force, for example: (a) transactions of business in securities on the stock exchanges are only through stock brokers who have been granted a certificate by SEBI, (b) every transaction is settled through a custodian who is under obligation to report to SEBI and RBI for all transactions on a daily basis, (c) provisions of SEBI's Substantial Acquisition of Shares and Takeovers Regulations, 1997 and (d) monitoring of sectoral caps by RBI on a daily basis.

2. Government of India, Ministry of Finance, *Budget Speech of the Union Finance Minister,* 2011-12.

Part II

Securities Laws

11

Securities Contracts (Regulation) Act (SCRA), 1956

SCRA regulates transactions in securities. The Act deals with recognition of stock exchanges by Central Government (whose powers in this case are delegated to SEBI), powers to suspend the business of stock exchange or supersede its governing board. It provides for regulation of contracts and options in securities. There are also provisions relating to listing of securities and right to appeal to Securities Appellate Tribunal in case of refusal by exchange to list securities of listed companies. Under the Act, there are provisions for adjudication proceedings to be conducted by adjudicating officer appointed by SEBI and imposition of monetary penalties for various violations. SEBI also has powers to issue directions against entities such as stock exchanges, listed companies etc. There are also provisions for initiation of prosecution proceedings under the Act.

Central Government has also issued Securities Contracts (Regulation) Rules, 1957 which, *inter alia*, contain qualifications for persons to be members of stock exchange, books of accounts to be maintained by members, listing conditions etc.

Stock exchanges in India are regulated and controlled by the Securities Contracts (Regulation) Act, 1956. The objects clause describes the Act as "An Act to prevent undesirable transactions in securities by regulating the business of dealing therein, by providing for certain other matters connected therewith".

11.1 Meaning of Securities and Government Securities

Under Section 2 of the Securities Contracts (Regulation) Act, 1956, securities include the following:

1. Shares, scrips, stocks, bonds, debentures, debenture stocks, or other marketable securities of a like nature in or of any

incorporated company or other body corporate.

2. Government securities.
3. Such other instruments as may be declared by the Central Govt. to be securities.
4. Rights or interests in securities.

Government Securities mean securities created and issued—whether before or after the commencement of the Securities Contracts (Regulations) Act, 1956—by the Central Government or a State Government for the purpose of raising a public loan and having one of the forms specified in Section 2(2) of the Public Debt Act, 1944 (since replaced by the Government Securities Act, 2006).

11.2 Meaning and Recognition of Stock Exchange

According to the Act, stock exchange means any body of individuals, whether incorporated or not, constituted for the purpose of assisting, regulating or controlling the business of buying, selling or dealing in securities. Any stock exchange, which is desirous of being recognised for the purposes of this Act may make an application in the prescribed manner to the Government (Section 3). The Central Government may grant recognition to a stock exchange if it is satisfied, after making such inquiry as may be necessary in this behalf and after obtaining such further information, if any, as it may require (Section 4).

If the Central Government is of the opinion that the recognition granted to a stock exchange under the provisions of this Act should, in the interest of the trade or in the public interest, be withdrawn, the Central Government may serve on the governing body of the stock exchange a written notice that the Central Government is considering the withdrawal of the recognition for the reasons stated in the notice and after giving an opportunity to the governing body to be heard in the matter, the Central Government may withdraw, by notification in the Official Gazette, the recognition granted to the stock exchange (Section 5).

11.3 Amendment of SCRA

In pursuance of the recommendations of the L.C. Gupta Committee, SCRA was amended in December 1999 to include derivatives within the ambit of *securities* and the regulatory framework was developed for governing derivatives trading. The Act also made it clear that derivatives shall be legal and valid only if such contracts are traded on a recognised stock exchange, thus precluding OTC derivatives. The government also rescinded in March 2000, the three-decade old notification, which prohibited forward trading in securities.

Derivatives trading commenced in India in June 2000 after SEBI granted the final approval to this effect in May 2000. SEBI permitted the derivatives segments of two stock exchanges NSE and BSE, and their clearing house/corporation to commence trading and settlement in approved derivative contracts. To begin with, SEBI approved trading in index future contracts based on S&P CNX Nifty and BSE-30 (Sensex) index. This was followed by approval for trading in options which commenced in June 2001 and the trading in options on individual securities commenced in July 2001. Future contracts on individual stocks were launched in November 2001. Trading and settlement in derivative contracts is done in accordance with the rules, by-laws, and regulations of the respective exchanges and their clearing house/corporation duly approved by SEBI and notified in the official gazette.

12

Securities and Exchange Board of India (SEBI) Act, 1992

The Securities and Exchange Board of India (SEBI) was constituted on April 12, 1988 as a non-statutory body through an Administrative Resolution of the Government for dealing with all matters relating to development and regulation of the securities market and investor protection and to advise the government on all these matters. SEBI was given statutory status and powers through an Ordinance promulgated on January 30, 1992. SEBI was established as a statutory body on February 21, 1992. The Ordinance was replaced by Securities and Exchange Board of India Act, 1992 on April 4, 1992.

In 1992, the Capital Issues (Control) Act, 1947 was repealed and the office of the Controller of Capital Issues (CCIs) was abolished. With this ended all controls related to raising of funds from the market. The move was aimed at enhancing the efficiency, safety, integrity and transparency of the market. Presently, issuers of capital are required to meet the guidelines of SEBI on disclosures and protection of investors.

12.1 Objectives of SEBI

SEBI has emerged as an autonomous and independent statutory body. Its legally mandated objectives are the following:

1. Protection of the interests of investors in securities.
2. Development of the securities market.
3. Regulation of the securities market.
4. Matters connected therewith and incidental thereto.

SEBI prohibits fraudulent and unfair trade practices, including insider trading. It also regulates substantial acquisition of shares and takeovers. In order to ensure protection of investors and to safeguard the integrity of the markets, there is a comprehensive surveillance system. Stock exchanges are the primary targets for detection of market manipulation, price rigging and other regulatory breaches regarding capital market functioning.

12.2 Functions and Powers of SEBI

The SEBI regulates and supervises the securities market through its various regulations, guidelines and schemes issued from time-to-time.

Powers and functions of SEBI—as the securities market regulator—have been laid down in the SEBI Act, 1992. SEBI also exercises powers under the Securities Contracts (Regulation) Act, 1956, the Depositories Act, 1996 and certain provisions of the Companies Act, 1956. It regulates the securities markets, securities market institutions and market intermediaries such as the stock exchanges, depositories, mutual funds and other asset management companies, securities dealers and brokers, merchant bankers, credit rating agencies and venture capital funds.

The statutory powers and functions of SEBI were strengthened through the promulgation of the Securities Laws (Amendment) Ordinance on January 25, 1995, which was subsequently replaced by an Act of Parliament.

The SEBI is equipped with the following powers:

1. Powers to register and regulate, inspect, enquire and investigate and undertake audits, and to cancel registration (though in this last case this applies to the mutual fund rather than the AMC); also to prohibit issue of an offer document including prospectus or advertisement.
2. Powers to summon and enforce attendance and examine on oath, inspect registers and documents, discover and enforce disclosure of books of account and other documents.
3. Powers to restrain from business, suspend, search, impound and retain proceeds, access bank data and attach

bank accounts, prevent alienation of assets and issue cease and desist orders.

4. Powers to require compensation to be paid to investors.

SEBI has the power to impose penalties for violation of the Act and Regulations made under the Act. The Act empowers SEBI to investigate, adjudicate, hold enquiry and prosecute. There are also general powers to pass directions against listed companies in the interest of investors or the orderly development of securities market.

SEBI has regional offices in five cities, viz. Mumbai, New Delhi, Chennai, Kolkata and Ahmedabad.

The experience of SEBI during episodes of market misconduct revealed many limitations in the legal provisions of the SEBI Act. In addition, the growing importance of the securities markets in the economy has placed new demands upon SEBI. On October 28, 2002, an ordinance was promulgated which sought to strengthen SEBI. This ordinance involved organisational strengthening of SEBI, giving SEBI more powers for investigations and penalties, and making clearer concepts like insider trading and market manipulations.

The regulatory ambit has been widened in tune with the emerging needs and developments in the equity markets. Apart from stock exchanges, various intermediaries such as mutual funds, stock brokers and sub-brokers, merchant bankers, portfolio managers, registrars to an issue, share transfer agents, underwriters, debentures trustees, bankers to an issue, custodian of securities, venture capital funds and issuers have been brought under the SEBI's regulatory purview.

12.3 Model Listing Agreement

Listing agreement is an agreement entered between a stock exchange and the company seeking listing of securities on the exchange. It contains various requirements and disclosure obligations that companies must follow to remain as listed entities.

The Model Listing Agreement has been stipulated by SEBI

and is reviewed and amended by SEBI from time-to-time.

Clause 49 of the Listing Agreement of SEBI requires the companies, who are listed, to comply with certain provisions relating to board of directors, audit committee, subsidiary companies, disclosures, report on corporate governance and compliance.

Stock exchanges are primarily responsible for ensuring compliance of various requirements under Listing Agreement.

Securities Contracts (Regulation) Act (SCRA), 1956 stipulates penalties up to ₹ 25 crore for non-compliance of listing conditions pursuant to adjudication by an adjudicating officer appointed by SEBI.

12.4 Appeals against SEBI Judgements

Those who appeal against SEBI judgements are heard by the Securities Appellate Tribunal (SAT) and can also go to the Supreme Court if they do not accept the Tribunal's judgement. The SAT has three members, one of whom is required to be the presiding officer who is a sitting or retired judge of the Supreme Court or High Court. The two other members must be of ability, integrity and standing with experience of corporate law, securities law, finance, economics or accountancy.

13

Depositories Act, 1996 and Depositories and Participants Regulations, 2018

Depository Act, 1996 provides for regulation of depositories in securities markets. The Act, *inter alia*, deals with rights and obligations of depositories, depository participants, issuers and beneficial owners. A depository needs certificate from SEBI for commencement of business. Under the Act, SEBI has got powers to call for information and enquiry, give directions, levy penalties and adjudicate. Presently, there are two depositories, viz. National Securities Depository Ltd. and Central Depository Securities Ltd.

13.1 Depositories Act, 1996

13.1.1 Objectives of the Act: The Act provides for the establishment of depositories in securities with the objective of ensuring free transferability of securities with speed, accuracy and security in the following manner:

- Making securities of public limited companies freely transferable subject to certain exceptions.
- Dematerialising the securities in the depository mode.
- Providing for maintenance of ownership records in a book entry form.

In order to streamline the settlement process, the Act envisages the transfer of ownership of securities electronically by book entry without making the securities move from person to person. The Act has made the securities of all public limited companies freely transferable, restricting the company's right to use discretion in effecting the transfer of securities, and the transfer deed and other procedural requirements under the Companies Act have been dispensed with.

13.1.2 Benefits to Investors: These are as under:

- **Speedy Transfer of Shares:** With the development of National Stock Exchange and the linking up of regional stock exchanges across the country purchase and sale of securities can be conveniently conducted between persons situated far away from each other.
- **Avoidance of Trading Risks:** Depository system take care of large number of risks involved in traditional trading involving physical transfer of shares.
- **Dematerialisation and Rematerialisation:** An investor holding share certificate can get it converted into electronic holding. Again if at some future date the investor wants to convert his electronic holding into share certificate, he is allowed such conversion which is called rematerialisation.
- **Indemnification of Certain Losses:** Interest of owner of securities under depository mode is protected as the depository takes the responsibility of indemnifying owner for any loss caused due to negligence of the depository or depository participants.
- **Low Brokerage Cost:** Brokerage cost in the case of dematerialisation is much lower than the cost as regards physical transfer of shares.

13.1.3 Right and Obligations of Depositories, Participants, Issuers and Beneficial Owners: These are as follows:

- **Agreement between Depository and Participants:** A depository shall enter into an agreement with participant as its agent.
- **Services of Depository:** Any person, through a participant, may enter into an agreement, in such form as may be specified by the bye-laws, with any depository for availing its services.
- **Registration of Transfer of Services with Depository:** Every depository shall, on receipt of intimate from a participant, registrar the transfer of security in the name of the transferee. If a beneficial owner or a transferee of any security seeks to have custody of such security, the

depository shall inform the issuer accordingly.

- **Options to Receive Security Certificate or Hold Securities with Depository:** Every person subscribing to securities offered by an issuer shall have the option either to receive the security certificates or hold securities with a depository. Where a person opts to hold a security with a depository, the issuer shall intimate such depository the details of allotment of the security, and on receipt of such information the depository shall enter in its records the name of the allottee as the beneficial owner of that security.
- **Securities in Depositories to be in Fungible Form:** All securities held by a depository shall be dematerialized and shall be in a fungible form.
- **Rights of Depositories and Beneficial Owner:** A depository shall be deemed to be the registered owner for the purposes of effecting transfer of ownership of security on behalf of a beneficial owner. The depository as a registered owner shall not have any voting rights or any other rights in respect of securities held by it. The beneficial owner shall be entitled to all rights and benefits and be subjected to all the liabilities in respect of his securities held by a depository.

13.1.4 Other Provisions of the Act: These are as under:

- A stock broker, in his dealings with the clients and the general investing public, must faithfully execute the orders for buying and selling of securities at the best available market price and not refuse to deal with a small investor merely on the ground of the volume of business involved.
- A stock broker has to issue, without delay to his client, a contract note for all transactions in the specified form.
- A stock broker must not disclose or discuss with any other person information of a confidential nature of the client which he comes to know in this business relationship.
- A stock broker must not encourage sales or purchase of securities with the objective of generating brokerage or commission.

- A stock broker should not deal or transact business knowingly, directly or indirectly, or execute an order for a client who has failed to carry out his commitments in relation to securities with another stock broker.
- A stock broker who deals with a client must disclose whether he is acting as a principal or as an agent. He must ensure at the same time that no conflict of interest arises between him and the client.
- A stock broker should have adequate trained staff and arrangements to render fair, prompt and competent services to the clients.

13.2 Securities and Exchange Board of India (Depositories and Participants) Regulations, 2018

SEBI notified the Securities and Exchange Board of India (Depositories and Participants) Regulations, 2018 on October 3, 2018 which gained immediate effect. The Securities and Exchange Board of India (Depositories and Participants) Regulations, 1996 (Old Regulation) stood repealed upon commencement of the new regulations.

13.2.1 Highlights of the New Regulations: These are as under:

1. Depositories to declare specific type of securities eligible for dematerialization.
2. Issuers to enter into agreements with depositories to enable the investors to dematerialize securities held by them.
3. There shall be continuous communication between the depositories, participants, issuers, issuers' agents.
4. A mechanism to be developed by depositories for protection of interest of the investors.
5. The interests of the beneficial owners against risks are to be protected by the depositories by applying adequate measures or through insurance.
6. There shall be co-operation between the depositories and the beneficial owners, issuers, issuer's agent, custodians of securities, clearing organizations for having an effective,

prompt and accurate clearance and settlement of securities.

7. Participants to execute an agreement with beneficial owners as per the specified manner by the depositories before acting as a participant on his behalf.
8. Every beneficial owner is entitled to have statement of accounts from the participants as per the specified format as may be agreed between them.
9. Participants to submit periodic returns to the SEBI and their respective depositories as per the format specified by SEBI.
10. Participants to ensure safety and security of records and data submitted to them by the investors, issuers etc.
11. Issuers whose securities are eligible for dematerialization to have agreements with the depositories.
12. Depositories to establish an Investor Protection Fund.
13. The procedure of dematerialization of eligible securities has been established under the new regulations.
14. Issuers or its agents to reconcile the records of dematerialized shares.
15. SEBI has the power to appoint an auditor to inspect or investigate, into the books of account, records, documents, infrastructures, systems and procedures or affairs of a depository, a participant, a beneficial owner, an issuer or its agent.
16. SEBI has the absolute authority to take any action against any issuer or its agent, whoever contravenes any provisions of the new regulations.

14

Companies Act, 2013

14.1 Background

The Companies Act, 1956 Act was in need of a substantial revamp for quite some time, to make it more contemporary and relevant to corporates, regulators and other stakeholders in India. While several unsuccessful attempts were made in the past to revise the 1956 Act, the most recent attempt was the Companies Bill, 2009 which was introduced in the Lok Sabha on August 3, 2009. This Companies Bill, 2009 was referred to the Parliamentary Standing Committee on Finance, which submitted its report on August 31, 2010 and was withdrawn after the introduction of the Companies Bill, 2011.

The Companies Bill, 2011 was also considered by the Parliamentary Standing Committee on Finance which submitted its report on June 26, 2012. Subsequently, the Bill was considered and approved by the Lok Sabha on December 18, 2012 as the Companies Bill, 2012. The Bill was then considered and approved by the Rajya Sabha too on August 8, 2013. After having obtained the assent of the President of India on August 29, 2013, it came into effect.

14.2 Significance

The 2013 Act introduces significant changes in the provisions related to governance, e-management, compliance and enforcement, disclosure norms, auditors and mergers and acquisitions. Also, new concepts such as one-person company, small companies, dormant company, class action suits, registered valuers and corporate social responsibility have been included.

An attempt has been made to reduce the content of the substantive portion of the related law in the Companies Act,

2013 as compared to the Companies Act, 1956. In the process, much of the aforesaid content has been left, *to be prescribed*, in the Rules which are yet to be finalised and notified.

The changes in the 2013 Act have far-reaching implications that are set to significantly change the manner in which corporates operate in India. The 2013 Act has introduced several new concepts and has also tried to streamline many of the requirements by introducing new definitions.

14.3 Main Provisions

14.3.1 Types of Companies:

1. **One-person Company:** The 2013 Act introduces a new type of entity to the existing list i.e. apart from forming a public or private limited company, the 2013 Act enables the formation of a new entity a 'one-person company' (OPC). An OPC means a company with only one person as its member [Section 3(1) of 2013 Act].
2. **Private Company:** The 2013 Act introduces a change in the definition for a private company, *inter alia*, the new requirement increases the limit of the number of members from 50 to 200 [Section 2(68) of 2013 Act].
3. **Small Company:** A small company has been defined as a company, other than a public company.

- Paid-up share capital of which does not exceed ₹ 50 lakh or such higher amount as may be prescribed which shall not be more than ₹ 5 crore.
- Turnover of which as per its last profit-and-loss account does not exceed ₹ 2 crore or such higher amount as may be prescribed which shall not be more than ₹ 20 crore:

  As set out in the 2013 Act, this section will not be applicable to the following: (a) a holding company or a subsidiary company, (b) a company registered under Section 8, and (c) a company or body corporate governed by any special Act [Section 2(85) of 2013 Act].

4. **Dormant Company:** The 2013 Act states that a company can be classified as dormant when it is formed and

registered under this 2013 Act for a future project or to hold an asset or intellectual property and has no significant accounting transaction. Such a company or an inactive one may apply to the ROC in such manner as may be prescribed for obtaining the status of a dormant company [Section 455 of 2013 Act].

14.3.2 Mergers and Acquisitions: The 2013 Act features some new provisions in the area of mergers and acquisitions, apart from making certain changes from the existing provisions. While the changes are aimed at simplifying and rationalising the procedures involved, the new provisions are also aimed at ensuring higher accountability for the company and majority shareholders and increasing flexibility for corporates. The 2013 Act has streamlined as well as introduced concepts such as reverse mergers (merger of foreign companies with Indian companies) and squeeze-out provisions, which are significant. The 2013 Act has also introduced the requirement for valuations in several cases, including mergers and acquisitions, by registered valuers.

14.3.3 Prohibition of Association or Partnership of Persons Exceeding Certain Number: The 2013 Act puts a restriction on the number of partners that can be admitted to a partnership at 100. To be specific, the 2013 Act states that no association or partnership consisting of more than the given number of persons as may be prescribed shall be formed for the purpose of carrying on any business that has for its object the acquisition of gain by the association or partnership or by the individual members thereof, unless it is registered as a company under this 1956 Act or is formed under any other law for the time being in force.

As an exception, the aforesaid restriction would not apply to the following: (a) A Hindu undivided family carrying on any business, and (b) an association or partnership, if it is formed by professionals who are governed by special acts like the Chartered Accountants Act etc. [Section 464 of 2013 Act].

14.3.4 Insider Trading and Prohibition on Forward Dealings: The 2013 Act for the first time defines insider trading and price-sensitive information and prohibits any person including the director or key managerial person from entering into insider trading [Section 195 of 2013 Act]. Further, the Act also prohibits directors and key managerial personnel from forward dealings in the company or its holding, subsidiary or associate company [Section 194 of 2013 Act].

14.3.5 Corporate Governance: The 2013 Act intends to improve corporate governance by requiring disclosure of nature of concern or interest of every director, manager, any other key managerial personnel and relatives of such a director, manager or any other key managerial personnel and reduction in threshold of disclosure from 20 percent to 2 percent. The term 'key managerial personnel' has now been defined in the 2013 Act and means the chief executive officer, managing director, manager, company secretary, whole-time director, chief financial officer and any such other officer as may be prescribed.

14.3.6 Accounts and Audit: The 2013 Act has introduced certain significant amendments in this chapter. It has also introduced several additional requirements such as preparation of consolidated financial statements, additional reporting requirements for the directors in their report such as the development and implementation of the risk management policy, disclosures in respect of voting rights not exercised directly by the employees in respect of shares to which the scheme relates, etc., in comparison with the requirements of the 1956 Act.

The 2013 Act features extensive changes within the area of audit and auditors with a view to enhance audit effectiveness and accountability of the auditors. These changes undoubtedly, have a considerable impact on the audit profession. However, it needs to be noted that these changes will also have a considerable impact on the company in terms of time, efforts and expectations involved. Apart from introducing new concepts such as rotation of audit firms and class action suits, the 2013 Act also increases the auditor's liability substantially in comparison with the 1956 Act.

Unlike the appointment process at each annual general meeting under the 1956 Act, the auditor will now be appointed for a period of 5 years, with a requirement to ratify such an appointment at each annual general meeting [Section 139(1) of 2013 Act].

14.3.7 Dividend: The 2013 Act proposes to introduce significant changes to the existing provisions of the 1956 Act in respect of declaration of dividend. The changes are likely to affect the existing practices followed by companies with regard to the declaration of dividend.

The existing provisions of the 1956 Act in relation to the transfer of a specified percentage of profit to reserve is no longer applicable and thus, companies will be free to transfer any or no amount to its reserves.

14.3.8 Revival and Rehabilitation of Sick Companies: Chapter XIX of the 2013 Act lays down the provisions for the revival and rehabilitation of sick companies. The chapter describes the circumstances which determine the declaration of a company as a sick company, and also includes the rehabilitation process of the same. Although it aims to provide comprehensive provisions for the revival and rehabilitation of sick companies, the fact that several provisions such as particulars, documents as well as content of the draft scheme in respect of application for revival and rehabilitation, etc. have been left to substantive enactment, leaves scope for interpretation.

The coverage of this chapter is no longer restricted to industrial companies, and the determination of the net worth would not be relevant for assessing whether a company is a sick company.

14.3.9 Corporate Social Responsibility: The 2013 Act makes an effort to introduce the culture of corporate social responsibility (CSR) in Indian corporates by requiring companies to formulate a corporate social responsibility policy and at least incur a given minimum expenditure on social activities.

15

Insolvency and Bankruptcy Code (IBC), 2016

IBC, 2016 consolidates and amends the laws relating to reorganization and insolvency resolution of corporate persons, partnership firms and individuals in a time bound manner for maximization of the value of assets of such persons, to promote entrepreneurship, availability of credit and balance the interests of all the stakeholders.

15.1 Need for Entrepreneur-friendly Bankruptcy Laws

There can be many reasons why an enterprise needs to close down—voluntary or forced by circumstances. The ease of closing down business is crucial for a good entrepreneurship ecosystem.

With globalisation and competition, the possibility of a large number of manufacturing enterprises not getting business, and having to close, has to be particularly catered to. The experimental character of entrepreneurship and the risks involved need to be understood so that an entrepreneur gets another chance in which he/she may do better. The business environment can be strengthened by reducing the bankruptcy stigma and facilitating re-starts. Unfortunately, a great deal of emphasis is placed on stigmatizing failure. The underlying message is that if an entrepreneur has failed once, he would not be given a second chance. A policy change is needed here. Unless there has been wilful default, surreptitious draining of resources etc., a failed entrepreneur may have actually learnt from his mistakes and become a good investment bet.

At a broader level, the bankruptcy laws should be designed to help viable companies in distress, and make closing and re-starting easier. Enterprises need insolvency procedures which recognise that viable businesses can suffer from temporary problems, e.g. an economy-wide recession. Such procedures should facilitate the necessary internal reorganisation and restructuring of debt. A key objective of the bankruptcy laws should be to help viable companies survive while safeguarding the interests of the creditors. This requires being able to distinguish quickly and at low cost between firms to restructure and firms to close.

The policies and institutions of an economy should provide adequate freedom to every person to enable him to pursue his economic interests meaningfully. Inclusive economies provide such freedom to pursue vocation, create a level playing field for good ideas to replace obsolete ones, and encourage scarce resources to pursue the most productive avenues. Such economies unleash and realize full potential of every person and thereby develop faster.

Business plans entail informed risk taking to compete and succeed. Either incumbents are displaced by new businesses or new businesses fail to carve out a competitive space for themselves. Either way, failure of some businesses is integral to a market economy. When a business fails, it needs to be resolved at the earliest and expeditiously. Any undue delay in commencement or conclusion of resolution may lead to exodus of key stakeholders and aggravate the failure, sometimes beyond repair. If the resolution is not possible, an orderly exit mechanism should allow stakeholders to recover their dues from liquidation proceeds of the business and free-up resources for reallocation.

In many countries reforms have taken place that allow insolvency of businesses to be dealt with in a comprehensive manner that enables revival or rescue before liquidation and winding up. Insolvency is treated as a commercial phenomenon requiring to be dealt with in accordance with commercial principles in a framework of fairness and equity. There is an independent institutionalized process of providing a grace period for businesses to deal with distress. This is intended to enable a revival plan if the business is inherently viable, puts all creditors on hold pending revival, gets business out of holding period if it revives or takes action on winding up if the business is non-revivable. Both personal as well as business insolvency are dealt with on the basis of similar principles with ease of filing for bankruptcy and securing of certain protection from creditor action once this is done.

15.2 Situation Prior to IBC, 2016

Unlike limited liability entities, where the liability of the shareholder is limited to the extent of the contribution made or due from him, in proprietorships or partnerships there is no separation of personal and business liability. When a business fails, not only do the assets of the business but the entrepreneur's personal assets also get attached to pay off business dues. Further, all guarantors of the small entrepreneur get personally involved and in the eventuality of failure they also get implicated.

Prior to the implementation of IBC, 2016, insolvency of business entities was governed by a host of outdated legislations. The focus in these laws was not revival followed by structured exit in case of failure, but on recovery of outstanding dues through a court-driven process. The relevant courts under the statutes were district courts which took their own time adjudicating the petitions and were apt to enforce the processes of seizing debtor's estates, appointing receivers and punitive remedies against the debtor including imprisonment rather than enabling any revival or turnaround. Indeed adjudicatory order on an insolvency petition under these statutes laid the entrepreneur open to action including arrest and detention in a civil prison as if business failure was a criminal act.

The existing legal framework for insolvency and bankruptcy was spread across multiple statutes and was found to be inadequate resulting in undue delays in resolution and thus rendering it ineffective, at times. In an economy growing at a rapid pace not only the credit delivery mechanism but also the economic culture surrounding it needs to be as per best global practice. Thus, there was need for an effective statutory framework to deal with insolvency and bankruptcy to facilitate development of credit markets in the country, encourage entrepreneurship, improving ease of doing business, facilitate investments, create more employment opportunities leading to higher economic growth and development.

A closure of an enterprise required, *inter alia*, legal compliances related to labour laws, taxation laws, power utility, water utility, municipal body, creditors, financial institutions etc. Even when the laws were clear enough on the requirements to be fulfilled, the implementation of the same was problematic for micro, small and medium enterprises (MSMEs).

There was no mechanism that rescued failed firms or released resources from failed firms to alternate firms. The resources did not move seamlessly from less competitive firms to more competitive firms continuously. This deterred optimal utilization of resources and dampened entrepreneurship.

The promoters stayed in control of the company even after default. The creditors were ineffectual in recovering their dues.

There was, thus, a need to streamline the procedures, reduce discretion and intermediation.

15.3 Bankruptcy Law Reforms Committee (BLRC)

BLRC (Chairman: T.K. Viswanathan) was set up on August 22, 2014 for providing an entrepreneur-friendly legal bankruptcy framework, as announced in the Budget Speech of the Finance Minister for the year 2014-15. BLRC submitted its Report and Draft Bill to the Finance Minister on November 4, 2015. Based on this, a Draft Bill, namely The Insolvency and Bankruptcy Code, 2015 was introduced in the Lok Sabha on December 21, 2015.

15.4 Insolvency and Bankruptcy Code (IBC), 2016

IBC, 2016 is the bankruptcy law of India which consolidated the existing framework by creating a single law for insolvency and bankruptcy.

IBC, 2016 is a one-stop solution for resolving insolvencies. A strong insolvency framework—where the cost and time incurred are minimal in attaining liquidation—was long overdue in India. IBC, 2016 is intended to protect the interests of small investors and make the process of doing business a less cumbersome process.

Insolvency and Bankruptcy Code, 2015 was introduced in the Lok Sabha on December 21, 2015 by Finance Minister Shri Arun Jaitley. It was referred to a Joint Committee of Parliament on December 23, 2015, which recommended it on April 28, 2016. The Code was passed by the Lok Sabha on May 5, 2016 and by the Rajya Sabha on May 11, 2016.

The Code received assent from President Shri Pranab Mukherjee on May 28, 2016 and was notified in The Gazette of India on May 28, 2016. It became effective in December 2016.

It repealed the Presidency Towns Insolvency Act, 1909 and Sick Industrial Companies (Special Provisions) Repeal Act, 2003, among others.

15.4.1 Key Features: These are as under:

- **Insolvency Resolution**: IBC, 2016 outlines separate insolvency resolution processes for individuals, companies and partnership firms.The process may be initiated by either the debtor or the creditors. A maximum time limit, for completion of the insolvency resolution process, has been set for corporates and individuals. For companies, the process will have to be completed in 180 days, which may be extended by 90 days, if a majority of the creditors agree. For start-ups (other than partnership firms), small companies and other companies (with asset less than ₹ 1 crore), resolution process would be completed within 90 days of initiation of request which may be extended by 45 days.
- **Insolvency Regulator**: Insolvency and Bankruptcy Board of India (IBBI) has been established under IBC, 2016 to oversee the insolvency proceedings in the country and regulate the entities registered under it. IBBI will have 10 members, including representatives from the Ministries of Finance and Law, and the Reserve Bank of India.

- **Insolvency Professionals**: The insolvency process will be managed by licensed professionals. These professionals will also control the assets of the debtor during the insolvency process.
- **Bankruptcy and Insolvency Adjudicator**: IBC, 2016 proposes two separate tribunals to oversee the process of insolvency resolution, for individuals and companies: (a) National Company Law Tribunal for companies and limited liability partnership firms and (b) Debt Recovery Tribunal for individuals and partnerships.
- **Procedure:** A plea for insolvency is submitted to the adjudicating authority (NCLT in case of corporate debtors) by financial or operation creditors or the corporate debtor itself. The maximum time allowed to either accept or reject the plea is 14 days. If the plea is accepted, the tribunal has to appoint an insolvency resolution professional (IRP) to draft a resolution plan within 180 days (extendable by 90 days), following which the corporate insolvency resolution process (CIRP) is initiated by the court. For the said period, the board of directors of the company stands suspended, and the promoters do not have a say in the management of the company. The IRP, if required, can seek the support of the company's management for day-to-day operations. If the CIRP fails in reviving the company the liquidation process is initiated.

15.5 Amendments

IBC, 2016 was amended in 2017 to prohibit certain persons from submitting a resolution plan in case of defaults, and to prohibit the sale of property of a defaulter to such persons during liquidation.

15.6 Insolvency and Bankruptcy Board of India (IBBI)

IBBI was set up on October 1, 2016 under the Insolvency and Bankruptcy Code, 2016. It has regulatory oversight over the insolvency professionals, insolvency professional agencies and information utilities. It writes and enforces rules for transactions, namely corporate insolvency resolution, corporate liquidation, individual insolvency resolution and individual bankruptcy under IBC, 2016. It is a key pillar of the ecosystem responsible for implementation of IBC, 2016.

In short, IBC, 2016 enables a firm to get in and get out of business with ease, keep striving for resurrection and new pursuits, undeterred by honest business failures. It reduces incidence of failure in two ways. First, the inevitable consequence of default in terms of insolvency proceedings prompts behavioural changes on the part of debtor to try hard to prevent business failure. Second, it reduces failure by setting in motion a process that rehabilitates failing but viable businesses. If rehabilitation is not possible, IBC, 2016 facilitates closure of businesses with the least cost and disruptions. It thus addresses business failures by reducing the chances of failure, rescuing failing businesses where possible and releasing resources from businesses, where rehabilitation is not possible and thereby promotes entrepreneurship. It improves availability of credit by: (a) preventing default, (b) recovering default from future earnings of the firm, post resolution and (c) recovering default from sale of liquidation assets.

IBC, 2016 enables the optimum utilization of resources, all the time, either by: (a) preventing use of resources below the optimum potential, (b) ensuring efficient resource use within the firm through resolution of insolvency or (c) releasing unutilized or under-utilized resources for efficient uses through closure of the firm.

By liberating the resources stuck up in inefficient and defunct firms for continuous recycling, the IBC, 2016, has completed the circle of freedom to enter, started by economic reforms since 1991, with freedom to exit.

16

Limited Liability Partnership (LLP) Act, 2008

LLP Act, 2008 provides for a flexible governance structure to be determined by the partners themselves by mutual agreement, easy compliance requirements in comparison to companies, combined with limitation of liability to the extent of the partner's contribution.

16.1 Salient Features of the Act

These are as under:

1. LLP shall be a body corporate and a legal entity separate from its partners. It will have perpetual succession. Indian Partnership Act, 1932 shall not be applicable to LLPs, since LLP shall be in the form of a body corporate.
2. An LLP has to be incorporated with a minimum of two persons. The Act does not restrict the benefit of LLP structure to certain classes of professionals only and would be available for use by any enterprise which fulfils the requirements of the Act.
3. The LLP will be an alternative corporate business vehicle that would give the benefits of limited liability but would allow its members the flexibility of organizing their internal structure as a partnership based on an agreement.
4. On registration, LLP shall be capable of: (a) suing and being sued and (b) acquiring, owning, holding and developing or disposing off property.
5. A person may cease to be a partner of a LLP in accordance with an agreement with the other partners or in absence of agreement with the other partners, by giving a notice in writing of not less than 30 days of his intention to resign as partner.
6. In the event of an act carried out by a LLP, or any of its

partners, with intend to defraud creditors of the LLP or any other person or for any fraudulent purpose, the liability of the LLP and partners, who acted with intend to defraud creditors or for any fraudulent purpose shall be unlimited for all or any of the debts or other liabilities of the LLP.

7. A contribution of a partner may consist of tangible, movable or immovable or intangible property or other benefits to the LLP including money, promissory notes, other agreements to contribute cash or property, and contracts for services performed or to be performed.
8. While the LLP will be a separate legal entity, liable to the full extent of its assets, the liability of the partners would be limited to their agreed contribution in the LLP. Further, no partner would be liable on account of the independent or unauthorized actions of other partners, thus allowing individual partners to be shielded from joint liability created by another partner's wrongful business decisions or misconduct.
9. An LLP shall be under obligation to maintain annual accounts reflecting true and fair view of its state of affairs.
10. Provisions have been made in the Act for corporate actions like mergers, amalgamations etc.
11. There is a provision of voluntary winding up as well as winding up by the Tribunal.
12. There are provisions for inter conversion of LLP into private company etc.

LLP Act has paved the way for greater corporatisation of the small and medium enterprises, thereby enhancing their access to equity and funds from the market.

17

Payment and Settlement System in India

17.1 Significance of Payment and Settlement System

Payment and settlement systems form the backbone of any economy. The spectacular growth in financial transactions has necessitated certain radical changes in the payments and settlement systems around the globe. The technological revolution in the field of electronics and telecommunications has helped to bring about sophisticated developments in the payments and settlement systems in many countries. A well defined payments and settlement system is, therefore, a crucial component of the financial infrastructure of any country.

Payments system provides the arteries or highways for conducting trade, commerce and other forms of economic activities in any country. An efficient payments system functions as a lubricant speeding up the liquidity flow in the economy and creating a momentum for economic growth. The payments process is a vital aspect of financial intermediation; it enables the creation and transfer of liquidity among different economic agents. A smooth, well-functioning payments system not only ensures efficient utilisation of scarce resources but also eliminates systemic risks.

Payments system assumes importance in the context of domestic financial sector reforms and global financial integration. The time value of money flows has increased sharply in view of the competing demands on the financial sector. Efficient, low cost cross-border payments flow helps to promote international trade in goods and services. Foreign investments (direct and portfolio) are encouraged by the availability of an efficient payments system. For these reasons, an efficient and technologically advanced payments and settlement system performs a vital infrastructural function in the economy. Reserve Bank of India (RBI) has, therefore, been taking measures to set up such an infrastructural set up.

The payment and settlement systems are at the core of financial infrastructure in a country. A well-functioning payment and settlement system is crucial for the successful implementation of monetary policy and maintaining the financial stability. Central banks have, therefore, always maintained a keen interest in the development of payment and settlement system as part of their responsibilities for monetary and financial stability. In India, the development of a safe, secure and sound payment and settlement system has been the key policy objective. In this direction, the RBI, apart from performing the regulatory and supervisory functions, has also been making efforts to promote functionality and modernisation of the payment and settlement systems on an ongoing basis.

17.2 Types of Payment

The requirements of a modern economy in regard to settlement of transactions are diverse and variegated and the needs of manufacturing, trade, and commerce activities involve large value payments over vast geographic distances. External trade with the rest of the world involves payments in different currencies. Payments can no longer be completed by simple cash transfer in such cases. Therefore, there arises the need for additional forms of payments, which can be facilitated with improved financial intermediation and expansion of financial instruments. Cheques and other paper based instruments and to some extent electronic instruments have become important modes of payment in recent times in most countries because of growing financial intermediation.

Individuals, business entities or governments issue cheques or other forms of order on their banks in discharge of their payment obligations. The recipients of these orders would then get the funds embodied in these payment instruments through their own banks. As the number of banks grew over time, the volume of instruments exchanged among them increased substantially.

Consequently, as also to have an orderly means of transfer of payment instructions among banks at a location or centre, a common set of practices and mechanisms of exchange had to be evolved. When instruments presented by customers of banks become payable at outside locations, special collection arrangements are set in motion to collect the funds. If the collecting bank has a branch at the relevant outside location, there would be no problem, but, if the collecting bank does not have a branch at the outside location, it will have to enter into correspondent banking relationship with another bank at the said outside location for the purpose of collecting funds.

The payment instruments which are routed through financial intermediaries involve book entries at various levels to transfer funds from one party to the other. The range of intermediation varies to take care of different situations. This may, for instance, consist of instructions to intermediaries to move goods coinciding with the movement of funds as in the case of a letter of credit. Or, the instruction could be for payment of specified sums of money to the bearer of a payment instrument, as in the case of a bearer cheque. In some cases, the payment instruments are negotiable in the sense that they can be transferred from person to person in lieu of cash. In yet other cases, both the ultimate beneficiary and the destination could be pre-determined. In all these cases, banks play a crucial part in conveying, transmitting and carrying out the instructions embodied in the payment instruments.

While doing so, these intermediaries have to settle among themselves the monetary claims arising from the execution of payment instructions. Thus, whenever non-cash payment instruments are involved, they are accompanied by a chain of related fund transfers as well as a stream of book entries and messages. Banks in turn need an intermediate agency such as the clearing house where these instruments can be exchanged and where the financial claims on one another can be settled through a settlement bank, which is usually the central bank of the country.

Clearing houses facilitate the exchange of instruments and processing of payment instructions at a central point among the participating banks. Clearing Houses-manual and paper based in many advanced countries have gradually extended their range of activities to include automated and electronic means for settlement of payment transactions. Such an evolution is also seen in emerging economies.

Banks, as crucial intermediaries in the payments stream, provide deposit accounts to non-bank agents (i.e. individuals, firms/corporate bodies) which are considered as liquid assets and facilitate payments transactions. Banks provide credit facilities so that such payments can be effected with lower working balances. Moreover, they act as conduit through which domestic and international capital markets provide resources to the commercial sector.

17.3 Payment System: Current Scenario

Payment system architecture in India is based on international benchmarks, and guiding principles. The Payment and Settlement System Act, 2007 provides a comprehensive legal framework for payment and settlement services in India for subjects like authorisation of payment system operators, netting and finality of payment and settlement. The payment system objectives of having a safe, sound, cost-effective and wide distribution network are being met in so far as the large value and countrywide payment and settlement systems are concerned. The grand vision is that cash dominant economy may transit to a predominantly non-cash dominant economy with non-cash transactions primarily in electronic mode, which is the international norm. The existing payment system is being constantly reviewed to suggest an action plan for orderly growth of the payment systems.

Since 2015-16, all segments of electronic payments, particularly retail electronic payments, have shown healthy growth both in terms of volume and value of usage. For example, real time gross settlement (RTGS) and national electronic funds transfer (NEFT) value registered a growth of 41 percent and 107 percent respectively between 2015-16 and 2017-2018, reflecting greater adoption of the system by all segments of users. Similarly, with increasing number of banks offering mobile banking services and driven by the growth in e-commerce and use of mobile payment applications, the volume of mobile banking transactions witnessed a growth of 92 percent for the period 2016-17 to 2017-18.

Card transactions have also grown significantly at both ATMs as well as at the point-of-sale (PoS) with the growth in debit card usage at PoS picking up significantly. The growth in volume and value of transactions using pre-paid payment instruments (PPIs) issued by banks and authorised non-bank entities has also been significant. The volume and value in immediate payment service (IMPS) has also grown significantly with the development of the IMPS as a multi-channel system providing various options to customers to originate transactions. Paper clearing, on the other hand, witnessed a marginal growth of 6.7 percent in terms of volume between 2015 and 2018.

Payment systems in India comprise electronic payment systems as well as paper-based systems. Another classification pertains to large value payment systems and retail payment systems.

17.4 Large Value Payments

The large value payment infrastructure comprises RTGS, high value clearing, and CCIL. Based on the criteria outlined by CPSS, the RTGS system and the high value clearing system have been identified as SIPS. The funds leg of the CCIL-operated clearing systems covering government securities, foreign exchange and money market settle in the RTGS system.

The Indian real time gross settlement (RTGS) system was operationalised in March 2004. The system started operations with four banks and settled only inter-bank transactions. Subsequently, the system was opened for settlement of customer transactions. It was operationalised for settlement of multilateral net settlement batch (MNSB) files from September 2006.

RTGS system is owned and operated by the Reserve Bank of India (RBI). The system works on a mainframe computer. Members are provided with a participant interface (PI), using which the participants connect to the system at the RBI through the INFINET. The message flow architecture in the RTGS system uses the Y topology. The members communicate through their PI to the inter-bank funds transfer processor (IFTP) which validates all communication and also does the *strip and store* function.

Upon successful completion of a transaction and receipt of confirmation from the RTGS, the IFTP forwards the complete credit information to the beneficiary member's PI. All communication between the PI and IFTP and IFTP to RTGS uses digital signatures (public key infrastructure) to ensure security.

The membership of RTGS is open to all scheduled commercial banks (SCBs), primary dealers (PDs) and others, as may be decided by the RBI. The SCBs are provided with Type A membership, primary dealers Type B and clearing houses Type D membership.

Except Type A members, customer-based transactions cannot be submitted by other members. Type D members are permitted to submit only net settlement batches for settlement under the RTGS system. Other banks and financial institutions can participate as customers of the direct members.

RTGS operations are governed by the RTGS Membership Regulations, 2004 and RTGS (Membership) Business Operating Guidelines, 2004. The members of the system agree to abide by these regulations and guidelines and any subsequent amendments to these documents.

The settlement of RTGS transactions takes place in the books of the RBI. For this purpose, members have to open a 'RTGS Settlement Account' with the RBI at Mumbai. This account is to be funded at the beginning of each RTGS processing day from the member's current account with the RBI, and at the end of the day, the balance in the settlement account is transferred back to the current account of the member.

Members are provided with collateralized intra-day liquidity (IDL) facility to tide over their IDL mis-matches. This facility is provided to Type A and Type B members only. The IDL facility utilised by the members has to necessarily be reversed by them at the end of RTGS day. Failure to do so attracts penal action.

In addition to IDL, the system provides many features for effective liquidity management by the members. These include message release method, queuing management and queue visibility. The Indian RTGS has adopted the FIFO rule for queuing. The system has a centralised queuing arrangement with priorities assigned by the system participant. The participant and system operator can change the priority of messages/revoke the messages in the queue. The system operator would alter the queue only in extreme situations. At the end of the day, all pending unsettled messages are cancelled by the system. The system has a multilateral offsetting algorithm to resolve any gridlock situations that may arise. This process can be configured to be invoked manually or automatically by the system. Since it is mainly a large-value funds transfer system, a floor of ₹ 2 lakh has been prescribed for minimum value of transactions that can be settled through RTGS.

There has been a substantial increase in the volume of transactions settled through RTGS. The inter-bank clearing at all the RBI centres have been migrated to the RTGS system. Further, multilateral net settlements from CCIL, viz. rupee leg of US dollar-Indian rupee settlement, funds leg of government securities settlement and funds leg of CBLO, and the retail net settlement systems operated by National Clearing Cell, Mumbai (MICR cheque clearing, high value clearing, NEFT and ECS) are settled in RTGS as multilateral net settlement batch (MNSB) files. The liquidity management operations of the RBI are also settled through the RTGS system.

17.5 Retail Payments

These include MICR/non-MICR cheque clearing, national

electronic funds transfer (NEFT) system, electronic clearing service (ECS), cheque truncation system (CTS) and payment channels like credit/debit cards, internet and mobile phone-based products.

To sum up, a safe and efficient payment system is a prerequisite for smooth functioning of the financial markets. The conduct of monetary policy in an effective manner requires safe and efficient payment and settlement systems to facilitate transfer of funds and securities between the central bank and other participants in the financial system. An efficient and stable payment and settlement system is also a pre-condition for inter-bank money markets and other short-term credit markets through which monetary policy is transmitted. In addition, developments in the payment and settlement systems that affect the speed and realisation/availability of funds for further deployment can influence the overall demand for money in the economy.

18

Credit Rating Agencies

18.1 Meaning and Importance

Credit rating agency means a body corporate which is engaged in, or proposes to be engaged in, the business of rating of securities offered by way of public or rights issue.

Credit ratings measure a borrower's creditworthiness and provide an international framework for comparing the credit quality of issuers and rated debt securities. Rating agencies allocate three kinds of ratings: issuer credit ratings, long-term debt, and short-term debt. Issuer credit ratings are amongst the most widely watched. They measure the creditworthiness of the borrower including its capacity and willingness to meet financial needs. The top credit rating issued by the main agencies—Standard & Poor's, Moody's and Fitch IBCA—is AAA or Aaa. This is reserved for a few sovereign and corporate issuers. Ratings are divided into two broad groups—investment grade and speculative (junk) grade.

The importance of credit rating, as a tool to evaluate credit risk, has increased in recent years. Credit ratings are extensively used by investors including large institutional investors like banks, mutual funds, financial institutions and provident funds while making their lending decisions. This is evident from the fact that increasing number of debt issuance in the private placement markets has been rated even if it is not a mandatory requirement. The credit rating agencies regularly disseminate information on new/outstanding ratings through print media. The list of rated entities and latest rating actions can also be accessed from the website of credit rating agencies. Established rating agencies also periodically publish data regarding the default statistics and rating migrations.

18.2 Credit Rating Agencies in India

Credit rating in India is relatively new, compared to the developed economies. The first rating agency, CRISIL, was set up in 1987. Credit rating was made mandatory for commercial papers and debentures from 1991—when ICRA, India's second credit-rating agency was established. Since then, the rating industry has grown significantly in terms of rated debt issued and subscribed, both at the corporate and retail levels (primarily fixed deposits).

The importance of credit rating agencies in India as information providers, which had been increasing, came to greater focus with the adoption of Basel II framework. The rating agencies in India face two constraints which impact their default statistics. One, they have a small base of rated entities. Two, they lack the geographical diversification benefits which the international rating entities enjoy. The processes and methodologies adopted by rating agencies in India are generally in alignment with those of the international rating agencies.

Moreover, despite the above two constraining factors, their default statistics may not be out of sync with the Basel trigger ratios. The domestic rating agencies are equipped to scale up their resources, when required, to cater to a higher demand for ratings consequent upon implementation of Basel II.

At present, the ratings in India are issue-specific and not issuer-specific. The rating agencies, therefore, are also working out methodologies for undertaking issuer ratings. It is, therefore, expected that with the implementation of Basel II in India, the proportion of rated entities is likely to increase over a period, providing the appropriate basis for risk discrimination in the system.

The rating system is required to undergo a validation process consisting of a formal set of activities, instruments and procedures for assessing the accuracy of the estimates of all material risk components and the regular operation, predictive power and overall performance of the IRB system adopted. In the validation process, the bank has to, on an ongoing, iterative basis, verify the reliability of the results generated by the rating system and its continued consistency with regulatory requirements, operational needs and developments in the reference market.

Achieving these objectives requires the performance of quantitative and qualitative analyses, the breadth and depth of which is modulated in accordance with the type and scope of the portfolios examined, the overall complexity of the bank, and the reliability of the environment under analysis. The validation instruments and methods need to be periodically reviewed and adjusted in order to ensure that they remain appropriate in a context of continually evolving market variables and operating conditions. The validation process shall not consist solely of a statistical comparison of actual risk measures against the related *ex ante* estimates, but will also involve analysis of all the components of the IRB system, including operational processes, controls, documentation, IT infrastructure, as well as an assessment of their overall consistency.

The validation process involves verifying compliance with the quantitative and organisational requirements for the rating systems. Specifically, this should include the following:

1. Assessment of the model development process, with particular reference to the underlying logical structure and the methodological criteria supporting the risk parameter estimates.
2. Performance analyses of the rating system.
3. Parameter calibrations, benchmarking and stress tests verification that the rating system is actually used in the various areas of operations. The results of the validation process should be adequately documented and periodically submitted to the internal control functions and the governing bodies and should specifically address any problem areas.

Non-availability of adequate information, lack of separate departments for bond rating in different type of industries and subjective analysis of qualitative factors are some of the main problems which obstruct the smooth functioning of the working of the rating agencies in India. The objective operationalisation of subjective parameters, development of an independent database for industry-specific information, periodic organisation of training programmes and seminars by financial experts to improve the skills of rating analysts and establishment of private rating agencies to increase the competition and their efficiency which could go a long way for improving the functioning of the rating system.

Table 18.1 lists leading credit rating agencies in India.

Table 18.1: Credit Rating Agencies in India

S. No.	Agency	Location
1.	CRISIL Ltd.	Mumbai
2.	India Ratings and Research Pvt. Ltd. (*formerly Fitch Ratings India Pvt. Ltd.*)	Mumbai
3.	ICRA Ltd.	New Delhi
4.	CARE Ratings Ltd.	Mumbai
5.	Brickwork Ratings India Private Ltd.	Bengaluru
6.	Acute Ratings and Research Ltd.	Mumbai
7.	Infomerics Valuation and Rating Pvt. Ltd.	New Delhi

Source: Securities and Exchange Board of India (SEBI).

Credit rating standards followed by Indian credit rating agencies seem to be rather lax, showing greater consideration for the *issuers* need than for the *investors* interests. They are not sufficiently forward looking, resulting in frequent downgrades, not long after the original issue. For this reason, the rating agencies have not been able to win the confidence of investors. This is partly due to competition among the rating agencies. There is a need for regular data on default rates of financial instruments rated by different credit rating agencies and also on migration to lower rating grades.

19

Protection of Investors

19.1 Investor Protection Fund

The stock exchanges have put in place a system for redressal of investor grievances for matters relating to trading members and companies. They ensure that critical and price-sensitive information reaching the exchange is made available to all classes of investor at the same point of time. Further, to protect the interests of investors, the Investor Protection Fund (IPF) has also been set up by the stock exchanges. The exchanges maintain an IPF to take care of investor claims, which may arise out of non-settlement of obligations by the trading member, who has been declared a defaulter, in respect of trades executed on the exchange. Measures of investor protection that have been put in place over the reform period have led to increased confidence among investors. [1] To improve the availability of information to investors, all listed companies are required to publish unaudited financial results on a quarterly basis.

A continuing increase in the savings rate of households suggests that there is no supply constraint in terms of financial resources that could be channelled into the equity market. After the exuberance of the stock market in the mid-1990s and its decline thereafter, a large number of individual investors took flight to safety in bank deposits, safe retirement instruments and insurance. Households in India have increasingly tended to prefer savings in the form of safe and contractual instruments as opposed to capital market based instruments. Although retail investors have started showing some increased interest in the equity market in recent years, there is a need to increase their participation further.

19.2 Investor Protection in Derivatives Market

19.2.1 Guiding Principles of Derivatives Market: L.C. Gupta Committee on Derivatives Trading in India recommended the following four guiding principles of derivatives market in India:

A. Fairness and Transparency: The trading rules should ensure that trading is conducted in a fair and transparent manner. Experience in other countries shows that in many cases, derivative brokers/dealers failed to disclose potential risk to the clients. In this context, sales practices adopted by dealers for derivatives would require specific regulation. In some of the most widely reported mishaps in the derivatives market elsewhere, the underlying reason was inadequate internal control system at the user-firm itself so that overall exposure was not controlled and the use of derivatives was for speculation rather than for risk hedging. These experiences provide useful lessons for us for designing regulations.

B. Safeguard for Clients' Moneys: Moneys and securities deposited by clients with the trading members should not only be kept in a separate clients' account but should also not be attachable for meeting the broker's own debts. It should be ensured that trading by dealers on own account is totally segregated from that for clients.

C. Competent and Honest Service: The eligibility criteria for trading members should be designed to encourage competent and qualified personnel so that investors/clients are served well. This makes it necessary to prescribe qualification for derivatives brokers/dealers and the sales persons appointed by them in terms of a knowledge base.

D. Market Integrity: The trading system should ensure that the market's integrity is safeguarded by minimising the possibility of defaults. This requires framing appropriate rules about capital adequacy, margins, clearing corporation etc.

19.2.2 Measures to Protect the Rights of Investors in the Derivatives Market: Investors' money has to be kept separate at all levels and is permitted to be used only against the liability of the investor and is not available to the trading member or clearing member or even any other investor.

A trading member is required to provide every investor with a risk disclosure document which will disclose the risks associated with the derivatives trading so that investors can take a conscious decision to trade in derivatives.

Investors get the contract note duly time stamped for receipt of the order and execution of the order. The order is executed with the identity of the client and without client ID order is not accepted by the system. The investors can demand the trade confirmation slip with their respective ID in support of the contract note. This protects them from the risk of price favours, if any, extended by the Member.

In the derivatives market all money paid by the investors towards margins on all open positions is kept in trust with the clearing house/clearing corporation and in the event of default of the trading or clearing member the amounts paid by the client towards margins are segregated and not utilized towards the default of the member. However, in the event of default of a member, losses suffered by the investors, if any, on settled/closed out position are compensated from the investors' protection fund, as per the rules, by-laws and regulations of the derivative segment of the exchanges.

19.3 Financial Literacy

Financial literacy is the possession of a set of skills and knowledge which allow an individual to make informed and effective decisions with all of his financial resources. Understanding basic financial concepts allows people to know how to navigate in the financial system. People with appropriate financial literacy training make better financial decisions and manage money better that those without such training.

Financial literacy focuses on the ability to manage personal finance matters in an efficient manner, and it includes the knowledge of making appropriate decisions about personal finance such as investing, insurance, real estate, budgeting, retirement and tax planning. Financial literacy also involves the proficiency of fi..ancial principles and concepts such as financial planning, compound interest, managing debt, profitable savings techniques and the time value of money.

The main steps to achieving financial literacy include learning the skills to create a budget, the ability to track spending, learning the techniques to pay off debt and effectively planning for retirement. These steps can also include counselling from a financial expert. Education about the topic involves understanding how money works, creating and achieving financial goals and managing internal and external financial challenges.

There are many advantages of financial literacy. Financial literacy helps individuals to become self-sufficient so that they can achieve financial stability. Those who understand the subject should be able to answer several questions about purchases, such as whether an item is required, whether it is affordable, and whether it an asset or a liability. This skill can help a person develop a financial road map to identify what he earns, what he spends and what he owes. This topic also affects small business owners, who greatly contribute to economic growth and stability.

The lack of financial literacy can lead to owing large amounts of debt and making poor financial decisions. Similarly, financial illiteracy may lead to making poor financial choices that can have negative consequences on the financial well-being of an individual. Financial illiteracy affects all ages and all socio-economic levels. Financial illiteracy causes many people to become victims of predatory lending, sub-prime mortgages, and fraud and high interest rates, potentially resulting in bad credit, bankruptcy or foreclosure.

Endnote

1. The World Bank in its survey of *Doing Business* has worked out an investor protection index, which measures the strength of minority shareholders against directors' misuse of corporate assets for his/ her personal gain. The index is the average of the disclosure index, director liability index, and shareholder suits

index. The index ranges from 1 to 10, with higher values indicating better investor protection. Based on this index, India fares better than a large number of economies, including even some of the developed ones such as France and Germany.

Bibliography

Bibliography

Ahluwalia, M.S. (2011), "Second Generation Reforms in the Banks: Major Issues", paper presented at the Bank Economists' Conference, January, New Delhi.

Banerji, S., K. Gangopadhyay, I. Patnaik and A. Shah (2012), "New Thinking on Corporate Debt in India", mimeo.

Basu, Priya (2005), "A Financial System for India's Poor", *Economic and Political Weekly*, No. 37.

Chattopadhyay, S.K. (2010), "RBI Working Paper on Financial Inclusion in India: A Case Study of West Bengal", Working Paper Series, September, RBI.

European Central Bank, "Report on Electronic Money", August 1998.

Financial Action Task Force (FATF) (2013), "Anti-money Laundering and Terrorist Financing Measures and Financial Inclusion".

Gopinath, S. (2005), "Recent Development in Forex, Money and Government Securities Markets: Account and Outlook", *RBI Bulletin*, August.

Gupta, Sanjeev Kumar (2011), "Financial Inclusion: IT as Enabler", Reserve Bank of India Occasional Papers 31, No. 2.

Jadhav, Narendra (2003), "Central Bank Strategies, Credibility and Independence: Global Evolution and the Indian Experience", RBI Occasional Papers.

—(2005), "Monetary Policy, Financial Stability and Central Banking in India", New Delhi: Macmillan India Ltd.

Kaveri, V.S. (2001), "Loan Default and Profitability of Banks", *IBA Bulletin,* January.

Malhotra, R.N. (1990), "Evolution of Financial System", Nineteenth Frank Moraes Memorial Lecture, Chennai, September.

Merton, R.C. (2005), "Financial Innovation and Economic Performance", *Journal of Applied Corporate Finance,*

Vol. 4, Issue 4, 12-22.

Metzer, S.R. (2000), "Strategic Planning for Future Bank Growth", *The Banker's Magazine,* July-August.

Nair, C.K.G. (2012), "Financial Sector Reforms: Refining the Architecture", in R. Malhotra (ed.), 'A Critical Decade: Policies for India's Development', Oxford University Press, New Delhi.

Puhazhendhi, V. and K.J.S. Satyasai (2001), "Microfinance for Rural People: An Impact Study", NABARD, Mumbai.

Rajan, R. and L. Zingales (1998), "Financial Dependence and Growth", *American Economic Review*, Vol. 88.

Rajaraman, Indira (2005), "Financing Rural Infrastructure in Developing Countries", *Applied Econometrics and International Development,* Vol. 5.

Rangarajan, C. (1988), "Issues in Monetary Management", Presidential Address at the Indian Economic Conference, Calcutta, December.

—(1997), "Activating Debt Markets in India", *RBI Bulletin*, October.

Reddy, Y.V. (1997), "Financial Sector Reforms and RBI's Balance Sheet Management", *RBI Bulletin*, December.

Reserve Bank of India, "Functions and Working of RBI", Fourth Edition (1983).

—"Report of the Working Group on the Money Market (Chairman: N. Vaghul)", 1987.

—"Report of the Committee to Enquire into the Irregularities in Securities Transactions of Banks and Financial Institutions (Chairman: R. Janakiraman)", 1992.

—"Report of the Expert Group on Foreign Exchange Market in India (Chairman: O.P. Sodhani)", 1995.

—"Report of the Committee on Capital Account Convertibility (Chairman: S.S. Tarapore)", 1997.

—"Report of the Advisory Group on Transparency in Monetary and Financial Policies (Chairman: M. Narasimham)", 2000.

—"Risk-Based Supervision Manual", 2003.

——"Report of the Working Group on Instruments of Sterilisation (Chairman: Usha Thorat)", 2003.

——"Report of the Technical Group on Money Market", May 2005.

——"Report of the Internal Technical Group on Central Government Securities Market", July 2005.

——"Annual Report" (various issues).

Sinha, Saurabh (1998), "Micro Credit: Impact, Training and Sustainability", Institute of Development Studies (IDS), Vol. 29, No. 4, October, University Sussex, U.K.

Srikrishna, B.N. (2013), "Report of the Financial Sector Legislative Reforms Commission", Volume I, Ministry of Finance, Government of India.

Tarapore, S.S. (1990), "Domestic Debt Management Policy and Monetary Control", 18th SEANZA Central Banking Course Lectures, Reserve Bank of India, Mumbai.

——(1996), "The Government Securities Market: The Next Stage of Reform", Valedictory Address at the Conference on Government Securities Market, Securities Trading Corporation of India, April.

Thorat, U. (2010), Keynote address at a panel session on "Setting New Paradigm in Regulation" at the FICCI-IBA Conference on 'Global Banking: Paradigm Shift'.

——(2002), "Developing Bond Markets to Diversify Long-Term Development Finance: Country Study of India", *Asia-Pacific Development Journal*, June.

Valpy, FitzGerald (2006), "Financial Development and Economic Growth: A Critical View", Background paper for World Economic and Social Survey, 2006, Oxford University, U.K.

World Bank, "Improving Access to Finance for India's Rural Poor", The World Bank, 2008.

—— "Finance for All: Policies and Pitfalls in Expanding Access", World Bank, Washington, 2008.

——"Measuring Financial Inclusion", Policy Research Working Paper, 6025, World Bank, Washington D.C., 2011.

—"Financial Access: The State of Financial Inclusion through the Crisis", Consultative Group to Assist the Poor (CGAP), 2010.

Websites

Ministry of Finance, Government of India
Ministry of Corporate Affairs, Government of India
Reserve Bank of India (RBI)
Securities and Exchange Board of India (SEBI)
Niti Aayog
World Bank
International Monetary Fund (IMF)
Bank for International Settlements (BIS)

Index

Index